HAIR

is a slender threadlike outgrowth
of the epidermis of an animal.

HAIR

long, straight, curly, fuzzy, snaggy,
shaggy, ratty, matty, oily, greasy,
fleecy, shining, gleaming, steaming,
flaxen, waxen, knotted, polkadotted,
twisted, beaded, braided, powdered,
flowered, confettied, bangled, tangled,
spangled, spaghettied

HAÏR

HAIR

The American Tribal Love-Rock Musical[1]

Book & Lyrics
by
GEROME RAGNI and JAMES RADO

Music by Galt MacDermot

Photography by Dagmar

PUBLISHED BY POCKET BOOKS NEW YORK

Another *Original* publication of POCKET BOOKS

POCKET BOOKS, a Simon & Schuster division of
GULF & WESTERN CORPORATION
1230 Avenue of the Americas, New York, N.Y. 10020

ISBN: 0-671-83071-6

First Pocket Books printing September, 1969

15   14   13   12   11   10   9   8

Trademarks registered in the United States and other countries.

Printed in the U.S.A.

TIME:
The Present.

PLACE:
New York City, mostly the East Village.

THE SET:
The bare stage, totally exposed, no wing masking and, if possible, the entire proscenium arch stripped of any curtain, thus exposing the fly area, the grid, etc. The brick walls, the radiator pipes, the stage ropes, the light-pipes, all lights, are visible, as well as the three flag drops—perhaps some costumes might be hung on light-pipes and flown.

The floor is raked slightly and should be made to simulate *dirt.*

There are two permanent set pieces on the raked stage. They are:

1. Totem Pole—stage right center—a large, authentic, beautiful American Indian totem pole.

2. A Crucifix-Tree—stage left center—a metal, modern sculpture Crucifix, with a rather abstract Jesus on it. The Crucifix also resembles a tree: the main cross branch, other smaller branches. Jesus is electrified with tiny twinkling lights in his eyes and on his body. At times, of course, the tree is climbed.

The stage hands, the stage managers, etc., will be visible in the wings (though the wings are not brightly lit).

In short, all of the elements of this production are contained within the stage area from the outset and are manipulated in full view of the audience as the play progresses.

Exterior scenes make use of the dirt floor. For the interior scenes, oriental rugs will be rolled out by The Tribe themselves. In fact, The Tribe will do most of the set changes, as simple as they are.

In summary, the set:
1. Bare, exposed stage
2. Dirt, raked floor
3. Totem pole and Crucifix-Tree
4. Drops to be flown in
    a. American flag—from 1776
    b. Another American flag—1776
    c. American flag—1967

The Sound will be rock music. It is very important that an excellent sound system be used that can regulate the balances of voice and musical instrumentation. The lyrics must be heard and for this reason all solo singers will probably have to wear chest mikes. Standard floor mikes will be used on occasion, as well, perhaps even in dialogue exchange for a specific effect. An engineer should be employed to control the balance through a master panel at the rear of the theater.

THE CAST:

The cast numbers approximately twenty-five. There are ten principals. Two of them—Mom and Dad—are about forty-five years old. They play six or seven different roles each, weaving through the play as the representatives of "the older generation." The rest of the cast is comprised of seventeen- to twenty-five-year-olds. All the boys have very long hair.

In addition, we will use huge puppets—ten feet tall, made in the form of policemen —(Tribe inside, manipulating them)—to hover in background at appropriate moments, as well as in the aisles. When not in use, they hang on hooks on the walls.

THE TRIBE:

The Kids should be approached, directorially, as a "tribe."

Marshall McLuhan describes today's world as a "global village." And today's youth is involved in group-tribal activity. So HAIR should be a group-tribal activity. An extension of what's happening. A coming-together for a common reason: a search for a way of life that makes sense to the young, that allows the growth of their new vision, however defined or undefined that may be; to find an alternative to the unacceptable standards, goals, and morals of the older generation, the establishment. (No matter that their task may never be accomplished, or that it may.) It's what's happening now.

The tribes are forming, establishing their own way of life, their own morality, ideology, their own mode of dress, behavior; and the use of drugs, by the way, has a distinct parallel in ancient cultures, in tribal spiritual tradition, both East and West.

The Kids are a tribe. At the same time, for the purpose of HAIR, they know they are on a stage in a theater, performing for an audience, demonstrating their way of life, in a sense, telling a story, in order to persuade those who watch of their intentions, to perhaps gain greater understanding, support, and tolerance, and thus perhaps expand their horizons of active participation toward a better, saner, peace-full, love-full world. They are trying to turn on the audience.

The entire opening of the show, for example, from the moment the audience enters the theater, is The Tribe preparing for the ceremony, the ritual, the war dance (the peace dance), the play—HAIR.

Note should be taken of the spiritual theme running through the play; outer space, astrology, the earth, the heavens, interplanetary travel, mysticism, as seen in the songs

"Aquarius," "Walking in Space," "Early Morning Singing Song," and "Exanaplanetooch," especially.

Also take note of the ever-present threat of the outside world on The Tribe, as expressed through the presence of the large police puppets, the projections on the walls of FBI, CIA, dark mysterious men, and Mom and Dad at times.

MUSICAL NUMBERS

ACT I

HAIR	Claude, Berger, and Company
MY CONVICTION	Mom
DEAD END	Sheila, Claude, Berger
DON'T PUT IT DOWN	Berger, Woof
FRANK MILLS	Crissy
HARE KRISHNA	The Company
WHERE DO I GO	Claude and Company

ACT II

ELECTRIC BLUES	The Leather Bag
EASY TO BE HARD	Sheila, Berger, and The Leather Bag
MANCHESTER (Reprise)	Claude and Company
WHITE BOYS	Dionne and Group
BLACK BOYS	Jeanie, Crissy, and Another Girl

———

Sixteen pages of photographs appear between pages 96 and 97.

HAÏR

ACT I

*The audience enters the theater. The Tribe
is already on stage, informal, dressing, putting on war paint, peace paint, dressed as
American Indians: headbands, beads, the
guys in loincloths, moccasins, beaded
dresses, etc. A small improvised tent is being pitched in the background. Some of The
Tribe wear blankets. Possible use of tribal
masks, colored greasepaints used freely on
faces. Rhythms drummed on old tin pots.
Occasional Indian yelps. Rising and sub-
siding drum rhythms from the band. Sur-
rounding the stage are all the props that
will be used during the course of the eve-
ning: stacks of newspapers, rolled-up rugs,
metal oil drums, old mattresses, toy props
that are used during the war scene, an um-
brella with "Love" painted on it in bright*

1

colors, sticks, poles, banners, balloons, flags, homemade improvised staffs with feathers on the ends of them, etc. The atmosphere of a primitive American Indian Camp at twilight. All looks quite primitive, tribal, and perhaps could be mistaken for another century were it not for the twinkling Jesus on the Crucifix. This is the Electric Tribe. *Bare feet, sandals, saris, loincloths, beads, old military uniforms, band uniforms, psychedelic design, incense, flowers, oriental rugs, candles, all combine to illustrate the emergence of a new-ancient culture among the youth.*

No overture.

Twilight in the Indian Camp. Drumming from tin pots, bottles, spoons, paper bags, metal objects, etc., and the band. Rhythm building. The Tribe is gathering.

SOLO VOICE

WHEN THE MOON IS IN THE SEVENTH HOUSE
AND JUPITER ALIGNS WITH MARS
THEN PEACE WILL GUIDE THE PLANETS
AND LOVE WILL STEER THE STARS

THIS IS THE DAWNING OF THE AGE OF
AQUARIUS
THE AGE OF AQUARIUS

THE TRIBE

AQUARIUS
AQUARIUS

SOLO VOICE

HARMONY AND UNDERSTANDING
SYMPATHY AND TRUST ABOUNDING
NO MORE FALSEHOODS OR DERISIONS
GOLDEN LIVING DREAMS OF VISIONS
MYSTIC CRYSTAL REVELATION
AND THE MIND'S TRUE LIBERATION

THE TRIBE

AQUARIUS
AQUARIUS

SOLO VOICE

WHEN THE MOON IS IN THE SEVENTH
HOUSE
AND JUPITER ALIGNS WITH MARS
THEN PEACE WILL GUIDE THE PLANETS
AND LOVE WILL STEER THE STARS

THIS IS THE DAWNING OF THE AGE OF
   AQUARIUS
THE AGE OF AQUARIUS

THE TRIBE

AQUARIUS
AQUARIUS

AQUARIUS
AQUARIUS

CLAUDE

(North Country accent)

My name is Claude. Claude Hooper. Claude
Hooper Bukowski. I'm human being number
1005963297 dash J, Area Code 609; maybe
you've seen me around. Just another number.
The most beautiful beast in the forest. I come
from Manchester, England.

MANCHESTER ENGLAND ENGLAND
ACROSS THE ATLANTIC SEA
AND I'M A GENIUS GENIUS
I BELIEVE IN GAWD
AND I BELIEVE THAT GAWD
BELIEVES IN CLAUDE
THAT'S ME THAT'S ME

NOW THAT I'VE DROPPED OUT
WHY IS LIFE DREARY DREARY
ANSWER MY WEARY QUERY
TIMOTHY LEARY DEARIE

CLAUDE *and* BERGER

MANCHESTER ENGLAND ENGLAND
ACROSS THE ATLANTIC SEA
AND I'M A GENIUS GENIUS
I BELIEVE IN GAWD
AND I BELIEVE THAT GAWD BELIEVES
  IN CLAUDE
THAT'S ME THAT'S HE
THAT'S ME THAT'S HE
THAT'S ME THAT'S HE
THAT'S ME

BERGER

(*Indian war whoop*)

Woo Woo Woo Woo Woo Woo Woo Woo
MANHATTAN BEGGAR
MANHATTAN GYPSY
MANHATTAN INDIAN

I'M A WHOLE NEW THING
I'M A LOT OF WILD
EV'RYDAY OF THE WEEK
I'M SOCIETY'S FREAK
I'M A FLOWER CHILD

MANHATTAN TOM TOM
MANHATTAN TATTOO
MANHATTAN TOMAHAWK

I'M A WHOLE NEW THING
A MUTATED BREED
I'M A PENNILESS HEAD
WON'T YOU GIMME SOME BREAD
TO FEED MY NEED

HASHISH
COCAINE
HEROIN
OPIUM
LSD
DMT
STP, BMT, A&P, IRT, APC, ALCOHOL,
CIGARETTES, RUBBER CEMENT, SCOTCH
TAPE, SAFFRON, SHOE POLISH,
MORNING GLORY SEEDS, COUGH SYRUP,
NUTMEG, ANN PAGE, DEXEDRINE,
BENZEDRINE, METHEDRINE, TWA,
S-E-X AND Y-O-U. WOW!

My name is George Berger. But I don't dig
George, so just call me Bananaberger. I know
you people think right off, oh, look, dear, isn't he
a cute one, what is it a boy or a girl?

(to a woman in the first row)

Hey, lady, can you spare a handout, something for a poor young psychedelic teddy bear like me? To keep my chromosomes dancing.

HUD

(dressed like a medicine man)

Comes the eclipse. I cover the white moon. I don't exist.

BERGER

More on Vietnam in a moment.

HUD

WALLA WALLA
GOOBA GOOBA

CLAUDE

(as interpreter)

Hud is mean
Hud is bad

HUD

WALLA WALLA
BOOGA BOOGA

CLAUDE

Hud whips women
Hud is happy

HUD

WALLA WALLA
GOONA GOONA
I'M A
COLORED SPADE
A PICKANINNY
JUNGLE BUNNY JIGABOO
NIGGER COON AND COTTON PICKER
MAU MAU AND UBANGI LIPPED SWAMP
    GUINEA

I'M
UNCLE TOM AND AUNT JEMIMA
VOODOO ZOMBIE LITTLE BLACK SAMBO
RESIDENT OF HARLEM
AND PRESIDENT OF
THE UNITED STATES OF LOVE

WOOF

And if you ask him to dinner, feed him:

HUD

WATERMELON
HOMINY GRITS

ALLIGATOR RIBS
AN' SHORTNIN' BREAD

CLAUDE, BERGER, WOOF

AND IF YOU DON'T WATCH OUT

(*Hud taps.*)

THE BOOGIE MAN WILL SHOUT

(*Hud taps.*)

HUD

BOOOOOOOOOOOO!

(*Stops tapping.*
Catholic Latin incantation by The Tribe.
Berger swings smoking Catholic incense
chalice.)

WOOF

(*holding out an imaginary bit of some-*
thing)

This is the body and blood of Jesus Christ and
I'm going to eat you.

(*He eats it, crosses himself, kneels, raising*
his right hand.)

I swear to tell you the truth, the whole truth,
and nothing but the truth so help me God, in the

name of the Father, the Son, and the Holy Ghost,
Amen.

SODOMY
FELLATIO
CUNNILINGUS
PEDERASTY

FATHER
WHY DO THESE WORDS
SOUND SO NASTY

MASTURBATION CAN BE FUN . . .

I'm Catholic, my name is Woof, and I refuse to
join the YMCA or sleep there overnight. They
advertise it as a Christian organization, but all
they have in the lobby are Protestant Pansies.
Pee Pee.

    (*drums under*)

HUD

I'm the Imperial Wizard of the KKK.

WOOF

I'm brainwashed people. Jesus Saves.

BERGER

I'm the Aluminum Coxman and you'll eat me up up up.

CLAUDE

I'm Aquarius—destined for greatness or madness.

HUD

I'M BLACK I'M BLACK

WOOF

I'M PINK I'M PINK

BERGER

I'M RINSO WHITE

CLAUDE

I'M IN ... VI ... SI ... BLE

(Claude, Berger, Woof, Hud join hands and start "humming" a chord. The rhythm from the band under this. The chord grows in volume, moves up in pitch, increases in intensity; The Tribe gradually joins in; the rhythm from the band becomes more rapid

and driving; the crescendo reaches its peak as the "Culpepper Minute Men" flag lowers rapidly behind the four guys. The flag: it is large, covers practically all the stage. It is a replica of an authentic American flag dating from approximately 1776. On it is a huge rattlesnake, coiled, ready to strike. Above it reads: "The Culpepper Minute Men." In the middle reads: "Liberty or Death." At the bottom reads: "Don't Tread on Me." The Tribe tapers off the chord rapidly as Claude, Berger, Woof, and Hud go into "Ain't Got No.")

WOOF	ANSWERS DIVIDED AMONG OTHER THREE
AINT GOT NO HOME	SO
AINT GOT NO SHOES	POOR
AINT GOT NO MONEY	HONEY
AINT GOT NO CLASS	COMMON
AINT GOT NO SCARF	
AINT GOT NO GLOVES	COLD
AINT GOT NO BED	BEAT
AINT GOT NO POT	BUSTED
AINT GOT NO FAITH	CATHOLIC

(The Tribe panhandles the audience.)

HUD	OTHER THREE
AINT GOT NO MOTHER	ORPHAN
AINT GOT NO CULTURE	MAN
AINT GOT NO FRIENDS	LUCKY
AINT GOT NO SCHOOLIN'	DUMB
AINT GOT NO SHINE	
AINT GOT NO UNDERWEAR	BAG
AINT GOT NO SOAP	DIRTY
AINT GOT NO A-TRAIN	
AINT GOT NO MIND	LOST IT

(*Claude has put on steel-rimmed reading glasses, takes out of his back pocket an air-mail edition of The* [London] *Times, moves downstage and kneels, spreading newspaper on floor, reading it. Stacks of newspapers all over stage. Mom comes downstage and begins dancing about Claude to a "Thirties-type melody," undressing as she dances, down to her slip and stocking feet, placing her clothes on the chair. Claude takes no note of her, continues reading. She continues the seduction.*)

CLAUDE

(*exorcism of the newspaper, affecting North Country English accent, Yoga lotus position, incense, pot smoking*)

"Hello there . . . ever thought how you're living smack bang in the middle of the Stone Age? This, folks, is the Psychedelic Stone Age. Without doubt, the most exciting time this weary, whirling, square globe has seen for generations. And it's *your* age . . . you are living it, you are psyching it, you are stoning it . . ."

(*He tears up pieces of newspaper.*)

MOM

I'm beat . . .

CLAUDE

"It's the age of electronic dinosaurs and cybernetic Indians and the daily News, the age where it's more fun than ever to be young . . ."

MOM

Did you see about that job today?

CLAUDE

"An age where it's more fun than ever to be stoned."

(*Claude tears up newspaper violently.*)

MOM

(*sarcastic, but still the seductress*)

Mountains of paper all over this house . . . your clippings, your magazines, your newspapers . . .

CLAUDE

(*cool British, reading from another newspaper*)

Got to keep up with the Times tra la . . .

(*tears out an article very neatly*)

MOM

Tear, tear, tear, you are nothing but tissue paper . . .

(*Music stops abruptly, as Claude, in a mock rage, attacks Mom, still with English accent.*)

CLAUDE

You save S&H Green Stamps and King Korn Stamps and bloody Plaid Stamps and box tops and Betty Crocker Coupons and Cut Rite and Kelloggs and soap coupons and Co-Op and God-knows-what coupons.

(*pointing accusatory finger*)

I've seen you pasting one regular King Korn Stamp in each thirty spaces on this page and pasting five *Big* Ten King Korn Stamps here and licking one *Super Bonus* King Korn Stamp for each fifty blocks on this page. You cut out, rip open, paste on, and save, and I am your lover, and I demand my civil rights, and there is . . .

MOM

Stop that. You stop that right now. We work hard for a living. Start being an American. Find a job. The trouble with you is you're not an American. All these Bolshevik ideas. It's disgusting. Look at yourself.

CLAUDE

MANCHESTER ENGLAND ENGLAND
ACROSS THE ATLANTIC SEA
AND I'M A GENIUS GENIUS
I BELIEVE IN GAWD
AND I BELIEVE THAT GAWD BELIEVES
    IN CLAUDE
THAT'S ME THAT'S ME

But I don't know how long me old man's gonna put up with that, do I?

MOM

He told me he's not giving you any more money.

CLAUDE

Oh, I've got to get out of this flat and start Liver-poolin' it up with me mates.

MOM

What are you going to do with your life? Besides dishevelled . . . what do you want to be?

CLAUDE

Kate Smith.

MOM

Start facing reality . . .

CLAUDE

Which one?

MOM

Your father and I love you.

CLAUDE

I was born right here in dirty, slummy, mucky, polluted Flushing.

MOM

Look at those trousers.

CLAUDE

I'm Aquarius and destined for greatness or madness.

MOM

So's your father. Don't shame us, Claude.

CLAUDE

Out onto the technicolor streets with me daffodils . . .

MOM

The Army . . .

CLAUDE

. . . me daffodils . . .

MOM

. . . The Army'll make a man of you . . .

CLAUDE

. . . tambourining it up and everyone lookin' at electronic me.

MOM

The Army.

CLAUDE

Stand aside, sergeant.

MOM

Or the Navy.

CLAUDE

I'm sleeping out tonight.

MOM

This is where it's at, honey, not out there . . .

CLAUDE

Carry on . . .

MOM

You will change your trousers before you leave this *home* . . . and take off my beads.

CLAUDE

Mother, it's embarrassing . . . the audience . . .

MOM

(*to audience*)

Hello there. This is not a reservation. Tonto!

CLAUDE

This is 1968, dearie, not 1948.

MOM

1968! What have you got, 1968, may I ask? What have you got, 1968, that makes you so damn superior and gives me such a headache?

CLAUDE

Well, if you really want to know, 1948 ...

I GOT LIFE MOTHER
I GOT LAUGHS SISTER
I GOT FREEDOM BROTHER
I GOT GOOD TIMES MAN

I GOT CRAZY WAYS DAUGHTER
I GOT MILLION-DOLLAR CHARM COUSIN
I GOT HEADACHES AND TOOTHACHES
AND BAD TIMES TOO
LIKE YOU

(*Mom now has tambourine and accompanies Claude.*)

I GOT MY HAIR
I GOT MY HEAD
I GOT BRAINS
I GOT MY EARS

I GOT MY EYES
I GOT MY NOSE
I GOT MY MOUTH
I GOT MY TEETH

I GOT MY TONGUE
I GOT MY CHIN
I GOT MY NECK
I GOT MY TITS

I GOT MY HEART
I GOT MY SOUL
I GOT MY BACK
I GOT MY ASS

I GOT MY ARMS
I GOT MY HANDS
I GOT MY FINGERS
GOT MY LEGS

I GOT MY FEET
I GOT MY TOES
I GOT MY LIVER
GOT MY BLOOD

I GOT LIFE MOTHER
I GOT LAUGHS SISTER
I GOT HEADACHES AND TOOTHACHES
AND BAD TIMES, TOO
LIKE YOU

I GOT MY HAIR
I GOT MY HEAD
I GOT MY BRAINS
I GOT MY EARS

I GOT MY EYES
I GOT MY NOSE
I GOT MY MOUTH
I GOT MY TEETH

I GOT MY TONGUE
I GOT MY CHIN
I GOT MY NECK
I GOT MY TITS

I GOT MY HEART
I GOT MY SOUL
I GOT MY BACK
I GOT MY ASS

I GOT MY ARMS
I GOT MY HANDS

I GOT MY FINGERS
GOT MY LEGS

I GOT MY FEET
I GOT MY TOES
I GOT MY LIVER
GOT MY BLOOD

I GOT MY GUTS   *(comments by The Tribe)*
I GOT MY
   MUSCLES   MASHKALUMBA!
I GOT LIFE   TELL 'EM WHITE MAN
   LIFE LIFE   MAHARISHI YOGI
   LIFE LIFE   LET IT ALL HANG OUT
                TELL IT LIKE IT IS
    MOM   HALLELUJAH
                   HALLELUJAH
And you got a lot   TELL HIM MOM.
of nerve, baby.

CLAUDE

AND I'M GONNA SPREAD IT AROUND
   THE WORLD BROTHER
AND I'M GONNA SPREAD IT AROUND
   THE WORLD SISTER
AND I'M GONNA SPREAD IT AROUND
   THE WORLD MOTHER
SO EVERYBODY KNOWS
WHAT I GOT

MOM *and* TRIBE

AMEN.
AMEN.

(*Mom exits. Claude runs back to game.*)

CLAUDE

AINT GOT NO SMOKES	SHIT
AINT GOT NO JOB	LAZY
AINT GOT NO WORK	
AINT GOT NO COINS	
AINT GOT NO PENNIES	HUSTLER
AINT GOT NO GIRL	HORNY
AINT GOT NO TICKET	
AINT GOT NO TOKEN	WALK
AINT GOT NO GOD	GOOD

BERGER

AINT GOT NO FATHER	DEAD
AINT GOT NO T.V.	HONEST
AINT GOT NO PIZZA	STARVIN'
AINT GOT NO GALLO	NERVOUS
AINT GOT NO SLEEP	HIGH
AINT GOT NO RHYTHM	WHITE
AINT GOT NO BOOKS	LOVELY
AINT GOT NO SOCKS	NASTY
AINT GOT NO SEX	UGLY

(*Berger sits in chair.*)

DAD

(*very pleasant*)

Well, Berger.

BERGER

(*rising*)

Yes, sir.

DAD

Sit down, Mr. Berger.

(*Berger sits.*)

Do you know why I called you in here today, Mr. Berger?

BERGER

I think so, yes.

DAD

We're getting to be well-acquainted, aren't we? You're a bad example for us here, Berger. And I must add you're not the only one. We've done everything to help you, persuade you, encourage you, and you've done nothing for yourself. You continue to make us promises and do nothing about it.

BERGER

Is that all, sir? Can I go now?

DAD

It's a shame, Mr. Berger. I don't understand all this.

BERGER

I hate your school.

DAD

You're such a bright boy and a good student.

BERGER

Screw *your* logic and reason. I'm tired of your *brainwash* education.

DAD

Mr. Berger, you may dematriculate in the front office!

BERGER

(*rises and goes, turning at door, rather English*)

Mr. MacNamara, this is 1968 not 1967. So long, love. Super . . . super . . . super . . . super . . .

(*He exits, standing facing audience down left.*

Dad, in a fury, picks up microphone to school intercom system, amplifying his voice.

Berger stands outside in the hall listening, motionless. Three bells ring—ding ding ding.)

DAD

Attention. Attention. This is your principal, Mr. MacNamara.

(*ding ding ding*)

All right, now, what is this school becoming? A costume party? Some kind of a giant festival dizzyland? Some students in this school have been ignoring PS 183's Personal Appearance Code, upsetting the morale of their classmates, distracting their fellow students, and I know the teachers feel their teaching is adversely affected in the presence of these apparitions. Well . . . one of your rebellious beatnik leaders has just been expelled by me. And let this be an ultimatum to the rest of you. This is World War III.

THE TRIBE

HELP!

AINT GOT NO HOME	SO
AINT GOT NO SHOES	POOR
AINT GOT NO MONEY	HONEY
AINT GOT NO CLASS	COMMON
AINT GOT NO SCARF	
AINT GOT NO GLOVES	COLD
AINT GOT NO BED	BEAT
AINT GOT NO POT	BUSTED
AINT GOT NO FAITH	CATHOLIC

DAD

(with whip and gun)

Mr. Berger.

BERGER

(growling like a lion)

Yes, sir.

DAD

Be seated.

BERGER

The girls love my look, they flock to me.

(All The Tribe, as lions, flock to Berger.)

DAD

We've become well-acquainted.

BERGER

I'm busy.

DAD

Bright boy.

BERGER

No thanks.

DAD

Fine student.

BERGER

Thanks, love.

DAD

Are you hopeless?

BERGER

Watch me!

DAD

We've tried.

BERGER

(*the last line as a lion*)

Channel 13.

DAD

I'm hip.

BERGER

Mr. MacNamara.

DAD

Mr. Berger, we do not send our chemistry teachers on trips. Your hair, your dress . . .

BERGER

(*now a cheerleader*)

Macy's Bargain Basement.

THE TRIBE

(*responding to the cheer, in Berger's rhythm*)

Macy's Bargain Basement.

DAD

But this, Mr. Berger.

BERGER

(*cheerleader*)

Call me Doctor Spock.

THE TRIBE

Call me Doctor Spock.

DAD

The last monstrous straw.

BERGER

Another chance?

DAD

Sorry.

BERGER

(*cheerleader*)

Oh, the social stigma.

THE TRIBE

Oh, the social stigma.

DAD

Further remarks?

BERGER

(*cheerleader*)

This is 1968, not 1967.

THE TRIBE

This is 1968, not 1967.

DAD

(*as a Nazi*)

You may dematriculate in the front office, Mr. Berger.

BERGER

(*"Heil Hitler"*)

Mr. MacNamara.

THE TRIBE

(*"Heil Hitler"*)

Mr. MacNamara.

DAD

(*to audience*)

General Hershey says draft 'em!

BERGER

Hell No We Won't Go!

THE TRIBE

Hell No We Won't Go
Hell No We Won't Go

DAD

President Johnson says call up the reserves.

THE TRIBE

Hell No We Won't Go
Hell No We Won't Go
Hell No We Won't Go
Hell No We Won't Go

DAD

Governor Reagan says turn the schools into concentration camps.

BERGER

Brainwash the masses!

THE TRIBE

What do we think is really great?
To bomb lynch and segregate
What do we think is really great?
To bomb lynch and segregate

DAD

Pope Paul says Stop the Peace Demonstrators!

THE TRIBE

NO NO NO NO NO
NO NO NO NO NO
NO NO NO NO NO
NO NO NO NO NO

Black White Yellow Red
Copulate in a King Size Bed
Black White Yellow Red
Copulate in a King Size Bed

Hell No We Won't Go
Hell No We Won't Go
Hell No We Won't Go
Hell No We Won't Go

What Do We Want	NO NO NO NO NO
Peace	NO NO NO NO NO
When Do We Want It	NO NO NO NO NO
Now	NO NO NO NO NO
What Do We Want	NO NO NO NO NO
Freedom	NO NO NO NO NO
When Do We Want It	NO NO NO NO NO
Now	NO NO NO NO NO

Peace Now
Freedom Now
Peace Now
Freedom Now
Peace Now
Freedom Now

AINT GOT NO GRASS   CANT TAKE
                     NO TRIP
AINT GOT NO ACID   CANT BLOW
                     MY MIND
AINT GOT NO CLOTHES YOU'RE FULL
                     OF PUSS
AINT GOT NO PAD   YOU'RE FULL
                     OF PISS
AINT GOT NO APPLES   WE GOT BALLS
AINT GOT NO KNIFE   CANT CUT
                     YOU UP
AINT GOT NO GUNS   WE GOT
                     BANANAS
AINT GOT NO   WHITE TRASH
   GARBAGE

CLAUDE

*(who has been burning a piece of paper
during the above)*

AINT GOT NO DRAFT CARD   BURNED
                         IT

THE TRIBE

BURNED IT BURNED IT BURNED IT
   BURNED IT

   ("Burned It" overlaps the following.)

AINT GOT NO EARTH
AINT GOT NO FUN
AINT GOT NO BIKE
AINT GOT NO PIMPLES
AINT GOT NO TREES
AINT GOT NO AIR
AINT GOT NO WATER
CITY
BANJO
TOOTHPICKS
SHOELACES
TEACHERS
FOOTBALL
TELEPHONE
RECORDS
DOCTOR
BROTHER
SISTER
UNIFORMS
MACHINE GUNS
AIRPLANES
AIR FORCE
GERMS

M-1, BANG BANG BANG
M-2, BANG BANG BANG

(*in unison*)

A BOMBS
H BOMBS
P BOMBS
Q BOMBS
CHINESE CHECKS
HINDUS
BINDUS
ITALIANOS
POLACKS
GERMANS
YOUSE
JEWS
UP AND DOWNS
ON 'EMS AND IN 'EMS

(*shouting to the audience now, out of
rhythm, overlapping each other, not in unison*)

VIETNAM, JOHNSON, HIGH SCHOOL, SEX,
COFFEE, BOOKS, FOOD, SCISSORS,
MAGAZINES, NEWS, CIGARETTES,
CANCER, LSD, 007S, SUPERMANS,
BATMANS, CASTROS, SUBWAYS,
CONEDISONS, HOLLYWOOD, NAPALM,
TUESDAY WELD, BURTON-TAYLOR, POP
ART, POP OFF, POPCORN, POPSICLE,

ANDY WARPOP, POP PAPER, POP UP,
POPEYE, POPPERS, LIPSTICK, DRESSES,
COMBS, GLASSES, LEATHER, SANDALS,
HARMONICAS, ENGLAND, OUTER SPACE,
ASTRONAUTS, JESUS, AIR, AIR, AIR, AIR,
AIR, AIR, AIR, AIR . . .

> (*Claude, Berger, Woof, Hud are gasping
> for air, as Jeanie, Crissy, and Dionne come
> forward.*)

JEANIE

WELCOME SULPHUR DIOXIDE
HELLO CARBON MONOXIDE
THE AIR THE AIR
IS EVERYWHERE

BREATHE DEEP
WHILE YOU SLEEP
BREATHE DEEP

BLESS YOU ALCOHOL BLOODSTREAM
SAVE ME NICOTINE LUNG STEAM

INCENSE INCENSE
IS IN THE AIR

BREATHE DEEP
WHILE YOU SLEEP
BREATHE DEEP

CATACLYSMIC ECTOPLASM
FALLOUT ATOMIC ORGASM

VAPOR AND FUME
AT THE STONE OF MY TOMB

BREATHING LIKE
A SULLEN PERFUME

EATING AT
THE STONE OF MY TOMB

WELCOME SULPHUR DIOXIDE
HELLO CARBON MONOXIDE

THE AIR THE AIR
IS EVERYWHERE

BREATHE DEEP
WHILE YOU SLEEP
BREATHE DEEP

    (*cough*)

DEEP

    (*cough*)

DEEP DEEP DEEP

    (*cough*)

I wired my parents for money . . . I told them
I was stranded. They said: Stay stranded.

DIONNE

That's Jeanie.

JEANIE

I live with a whole bunch of people on Teeny
Bopper Island . . .

DIONNE

She loves Claude.

JEANIE

Third Street and Avenue C.
Claude is my acid.
Claude is my trip.
Methedrine's a bad scene.
And Claude loves me.

> (*Angela, Crissy, and Dionne shake their
> heads behind her back. They exit.*
>
> *The Culpepper Minute Men flag is pulled
> back and we are in The Intergalactic Bath-
> tub—there is a sign which designates this
> tribal hangout.*
>
> *As a yellow bathtub and oriental rug are
> being rolled out, the kids sing and dance.*)

[*Note: Mom and Dad sit at an upstage table perhaps, facing the action on the stage, and react as an extension of the audience.*]

THE TRIBE

LBJ TOOK THE IRT
DOWN TO 4TH STREET USA

WHEN HE GOT THERE WHAT DID HE
   SEE
THE YOUTH OF AMERICA ON LSD

LBJ	IRT
USA	LSD

LSD	LBJ
FBI	CIA

FBI	CIA
LSD	LBJ

(*Berger enters.*)

WOOF

(*reading a nudist pornography magazine*)

Berger!

BERGER

Woof!

HUD

Berger!

BERGER

Hud!

(*English accent*)

Claude here yet?

HUD

No.

(*Berger jumps. Takes his key from his
pocket*)

BERGER

(*the height of cool*)

He entered. He locked the door. He checked
out the scene. He put his right hand on his left
breast and stretched his left arm high above his
head, waving to his blue-eyed soul brothers with
a smile. A hush came over the room—

(*Italian accent*)

Ladies and gentlemen, listen, when I drop-a

dead, when-a my heart-a go pzzzzzzzzt, like-a
this, I want to be buried in a bronze-a casket,
beautiful-a bronze, no clothes, nothing, put-a me
down stomach first, like-a this, everybody come-a
see me, they come-a kiss-a my ass.

He put out his hand and said: "Lay me five,
man, I'm free like a cockroach."

WOOF

(*skinning Berger's hand*)

I'm screwed up like a nudist.

BERGER

Blowing his cool, he said . . .

(*Now he bursts with excitement.*)

Woof, Woof, baby, Hud . . . I finally got out.
Out. Out.

WOOF

Out of who?

BERGER

ME AND LUCIFER
LUCIFER AND ME

JUST LIKE THE ANGEL THAT FELL
BANISHED FOREVER TO HELL
TODAY HAVE I BEEN EXPELLED
FROM HIGH SCHOOL HEAVEN

ELEVATOR GOING DOWN
GOING DOWN
GOING DOWN

EVERYBODY GOING DOWN
GOING DOWN
GOING DOWN

THIS IS MY DOOM, MY HUMILIATION
OCTOBER, NOT JUNE, AND IT'S SUMMER
   VACATION
SUCH A DISGRACE, HOW CAN I FACE
   THE NATION
WHY SHOULD THIS PAIN BRING ME
   SUCH STRANGE ELATION

ESCALATOR GOING DOWN
GOING DOWN
GOING DOWN

EVERYBODY GOING DOWN
GOING DOWN
GOING DOWN

EMANCIPATION PROCLAMATION
OH DR. LINCOLN MY HEAD NEEDS
  SHRINKIN'
LU LU LU LU LU LU LU LU LU LU LU
  LUCIFER AND ME
DOOMED FROM HERE TO ETERNITY
BAA BAA BAA

GROWING UP GOING DOWN
GOING DOWN
GOING DOWN

GROWING UP GOING DOWN
GOING DOWN
GOING DOWN

FORGIVE ME IF I DON'T CRY
IT'S LIKE THE FOURTH OF JULY
THANK GOD THAT ANGELS CAN FLY
FROM HIGH SCHOOL HEAVEN

EVERYBODY GOING DOWN
GOING DOWN
GOING DOWN

THANK GOD THAT ANGELS CAN FLY
FROM HIGH SCHOOL HEAVEN

EVERYBODY GOING DOWN
GOING DOWN
GOING DOWN

THANK GOD THAT ANGELS CAN FLY
FROM HIGH SCHOOL HEAVEN

> (*Amos 'n' Andy dialect*)

Waiter, waiter.

HUD

> (*very British*)

Oh, yes, sir. You rang, sir? What is the master's pleasure this time?

BERGER

> (*pointing to various objects all over the stage*)

I'll have one of those and one of those and that and that and that over there and this over here and that way over there and one of those one of those that and that and . . . YOU!

> (*Berger empties small bottle of pills on the table.*)

HUD

(*still British*)

Oh, yes, sir. Three cups of blood.

BERGER

And make it fast.

HUD

You see the color of my skin. It's white, sir. And you remember that. It's white, white, white. I'm no slave of yours. I'm white.

(*goes to get three cups of coffee*)

WOOF

(*upper British accent*)

Digger Digger
Dirty Nigger
Digger Nigger
Pull the Trigger
Nigger Nigger
Grows it Bigger

HUD

Oh, yes, sir, and don't you forget it.

(*Behind the next The Tribe sing softly.*)

THE TRIBE

EVERYBODY GOING UP
GOING UP
GOING UP

EVERYBODY GOING UP
GOING UP
GOING UP
ETC.

BERGER

(*dividing the pills into three piles*)

One for Billy Graham, one for Prince Philip, and one for Joe Louis. One for Cardinal Spellman, one for Rabbi Schultz, one for Mohammed Ali. One for Shirley Temple, one for Ronald Reagan, and one for Miss Rheingold.

(*Woof starts to drink.*)

BERGER

Uh-uh-uh-uh-uh-uh! Not yet hophead.

(*Bronx Jewish accent*)

My daughter. Let me tell you about my daughter. She sees flying saucers and monsters and all sorts of these things. And now she's floating around in that San Francisco somewhere . . . and all because of these pills.

Oy!

BERGER

(*He toasts.*)
Up PS 183.

HUD

Blood in your eye.

BERGER

Hud, can I pitch my tent here tonight?

HUD

Feel free.

WOOF

I gotta kick this drug bag. It's a bad scene.

BERGER

I don't care if you hate me for telling you this,
but you've got bad breath.

WOOF

Can I sleep with you tonight, Berger?

BERGER

Sure. Come on in. And, Woof, don't tell Claude about school; let me tell him.

(*to audience—very square*)

High School Dropouts: Dial OR 7-7390 for our Free Booklet telling how you can get your diploma learning at home-a. This is a recording.

(*Claude enters.*)

CLAUDE

This is Claude's day.

BERGER

Claudio!

(*Claude does not move.*)

Wait wait wait . . . don't tell me.

(*Claude and Berger and Woof and Hud nod heads simultaneously.*)

WOOF

No kidding.

BERGER

Aw, Claude, that's death, man . . .

HUD

Tough luck, baby . . .

CLAUDE

I've thought it over . . . I'll tell them I'm a faggot and hide out in Toronto.

> (*Claude picks up battery-powered megaphone, speaks into it, reading from his notebooks, first pantomiming taking a drag from a stick of marijuana.*)

"Ode to a Stick"
Poem
by Pfc Claude Hooper Bukowski

> (*electronic beeps, blurps, bells, and tinkles in background*)

Pick up my glowworm

> (*another drag*)

My little magic fellow
My little block of gold
My little blue flame
My little cloud in the sky
My little poison ivy
My little nonconformist
My little American bird
My little magic flower
My little electricity blowhole
My little white erection

My little garden of heaven
My little high above the tree castle
My little village far below
My little rug of grass
My little sunny balloon farm
My little growing on the hills
My little daybreak crumbles away
My little weird weed
My little Sunday breeze
My little raft of wood
My little naked tree
My little streak across the sky
My little special sunset
My little raindrop bed
My little whisper to the world
My little beautiful thing
My little swallow me
My little wrinkled old man
My little lord of the rings

(*another drag*)

Pick up my glowworm.

BERGER

The doctors dug your body, huh.

CLAUDE

They're hot for my ding dong.

BERGER

Didn't you tell them you're going to Pratt next year?

CLAUDE

(*English*)

They're queer for me gear. They flipped. Next year means shit. I'm not going in. I'll eat it first. I'm not.

WOOF

Eat what?

CLAUDE

My draft card.

BERGER

I thought you burned it.

CLAUDE

That was my driver's license.

WOOF

Eat it on CBS television.

CLAUDE

Berger, help me, how am I gonna get out of going?

BERGER

Dance bare-assed down Forty-second Street.

WOOF

Tell them you're a closet queen.

HUD

Shave your armpits.

CLAUDE

Com'on what am I gonna do?

BERGER

(*English*)

Do you think homosexuality is here to stay, love?

CLAUDE

Yes, dear, until something better comes along.

BERGER

Take me with you, tell them I'm your girl friend and you can't sleep without me.

HUD

Bet the induction officer your cock is bigger than his.

BERGER

Tell them your mother volunteered to fight in your place.

WOOF

Do they know she's a Viet Cong?

HUD

Uncle Sambo Wants You!

CLAUDE

(*to audience*)

I want to be over here doing the things they're defending over there.

(*starts to burn a card*)

BERGER

Become a nun.

HUD

Wet the bed, baby.

CLAUDE

They're not gonna cut it off.

BERGER

(*reading the burning card in Claude's hand*)

Mr. Claude Hooper Bukowski—New York Public Library.

CLAUDE

Berger, help me, no kidding around . . . if they draft me, I'll get killed or a leg shot off or something . . . I know it . . . they're not gonna get me . . .

BERGER

Oh, yes they are. You will go, and you will get killed and rape and loot; you will do exactly what THEY tell you to do.

CLAUDE

It's not funny, Berg . . . I'm not going . . . it took me years to get it like this, and I'm not gonna let them do it.

BERGER

Five years in prison at hard labor.

CLAUDE

I don't want to die.

THE TRIBE

AHHH!

(*"The Caissons Go Rolling Along"*)

LIFT YOUR SKIRT POINT YOUR TOE
VOLUNTEER FOR THE USO
BAKE COOKIES AND PIES FOR OUR
    GUYS

BERGER, WOOF, HUD

LIFT YOUR SKIRT POINT YOUR TOE
VOLUNTEER FOR THE USO
BAKE COOKIES AND PIES FOR OUR
    GUYS

(*Berger asks woman in the audience for lipstick.*)

(*"Anchors Aweigh"*)

YOUR LEGS SHAVE THE HAIR OFF
YOUR EYEBROWS PLUCK 'EM
REFUSE TO TAKE YOUR UNDERWEAR
    OFF

AND IF THEY MAKE YOU PUCKER YOUR
   LIPS UP AND PUCK 'EM

   (*"The Marine Hymn"*)

YOU'LL FORGET YOUR RUBY TUESDAY,
   YOU'LL FORGET MICHELLE YOUR
   BELLE
AS FOR LOVELY RITA METER MAID

   (*Berger puts lipstick on Claude.*)

   WELL SHE CAN GO TO HELL
EVEN MOTHER SWEET CANNOT
   COMPETE
WITH THE NEATEST PIECE WE'VE SEEN
CLAUDINE HOOPER BUKOWSKI
SHE'S THE QUEEN OF THE UNITED
   STATES MARINES
NERVOUS NELLIE

   (*Mom and Dad, who have gotten up from
the back table, approach the young men.
Mom is dominant; Dad has a camera and a
pad and pencil and takes notes.*)

MOM

   (*to Claude*)

Young man, excuse me. May I introduce myself.

   (*She hands Claude a Kleenex. He removes
his lipstick.*)

Here's my card. I did overhear just a wee portion of your conversation, and I would like to ask you a question, if you wouldn't mind.

CLAUDE

Sure, of course, what is it?

MOM

Well . . .

(*She giggles.*)

. . . this may sound a bit naïve . . . foolish . . . oh, my, I don't know why I feel so embarrassed . . . I . . . being a visitor from another generation like myself . . .

CLAUDE

Cool it.

(*She fans herself, using her hand.*)

What would you like to know?

MOM

Well . . . why? . . . I mean . . . why? Why?

(*She climbs up on chair Claude is sitting in, straddling him.*)

Why? Why?

(*Berger places another poster against the counter: "Ronald Reagan Is a Lesbian."*)

CLAUDE

You mean this?

(*holds up a strand of his own hair, while putting his arms around Mom's legs; outrageous orgiastic actions*)

MOM

(*rubbing her hands through Claude's hair*)

Yes . . . why that? I mean is it because you're a . . . oh, dear . . . Are you? . . . please forgive me . . . are you . . . a . . . Hippie?

(*She caresses Claude passionately as the stage falls apart. Glitter dust is thrown by The Tribe, bells, horns, rattles, great reaction to "the magic word."*)

BERGER

Is the Pope Catholic?

DAD

(*A timid soul, but he sits on the floor, grabs hold of Claude's leg and begins pushing trouser leg up.*)

Who are your heroes?

(*Woof displays a poster he has made:
"Jesus Was a Catholic."*)

BERGER

Medusa.

(*He embraces Mom who kisses him.*)

DAD

(*rubbing Claude's leg while grabbing for
his wife*)

Aa-ha!

HUD

Wonder Woman.

WOOF

(*trying to climb up on the chair too*)

Prince Valiant.

DAD

Aa-ha!

BERGER

Orphanie Annie.

CLAUDE

Vernica Lake.

DAD

Oh-ho!

HUD

(*who does not have long hair, of course, joins the throng of intertwined bodies*)

It's very simple . . . you ask me why? Like I like the feel of the silky strands on my ears and the back of my neck and on my shoulders. Goose-bump time, know what I mean?

MOM

That's very interesting.

(*to Dad*)

You see, he does it for the sensual experience.

(*now caressing Hud passionately*)

That's why . . .   HUD
That's why
That's why   (*to Dad*)
That's why   You dig my Dixie Peach?
That's why
That's why   DAD

                          I dig your Dixie Peach!

(*Poster: "Hair"*)

CLAUDE

(*breaks up the orgy with the start of his singing . . . or perhaps the orgy could continue into song*)

SHE ASKS ME WHY

Don't ask me!

I'M JUST A HAIRY GUY
I'M HAIRY NOON AND NIGHT
HAIR THAT'S A FRIGHT

I'M HAIRY HIGH AND LOW
DON'T ASK ME WHY—DON'T KNOW

IT'S NOT FOR LACK OF BREAD
LIKE THE GRATEFUL DEAD

DARLIN'
GIVE ME A HEAD WITH HAIR
LONG BEAUTIFUL HAIR
SHINING GLEAMING STREAMING
FLAXEN WAXEN

GIVE ME DOWN TO THERE HAIR
SHOULDER-LENGTH OR LONGER
AS LONG AS GOD CAN GROW IT
FLOW IT
SHOW IT

HAIR HAIR
HAIR HAIR HAIR
HAIR HAIR HAIR

FLOW IT
SHOW IT
LONG AS GOD CAN GROW IT
MY HAIR

LET IT FLY IN THE BREEZE
AND GET CAUGHT IN THE TREES
GIVE A HOME TO THE FLEAS
IN MY HAIR

A HOME FOR FLEAS
A HIVE FOR BEES
A NEST FOR BIRDS
THERE AINT NO WORDS
FOR THE BEAUTY THE SPLENDOR
THE WONDER OF MY

HAIR HAIR
HAIR HAIR HAIR
HAIR HAIR HAIR

FLOW IT
SHOW IT
LONG AS GOD CAN GROW IT
MY HAIR

I WANT IT LONG STRAIGHT CURLY
  FUZZY
SNAGGY SHAGGY RATTY MATTY
OILY GREASY FLEECY
SHINING GLEAMING STREAMING
FLAXEN WAXEN
KNOTTED POLKADOTTED
TWISTED BEADED BRAIDED
POWDERED FLOWERED AND
  CONFETTIED
BANGLED TANGLED SPANGLED AND
  SPAGHETTIED

OH SAY YOU CAN SEE MY EYES
IF YOU CAN
THEN MY HAIR'S TOO SHORT

DOWN TO HERE
DOWN TO THERE
DOWN TO WHERE
IT STOPS BY ITSELF

DOO DOO DOO DOO DOO DOO DOO DOO
  DOO DOO
DOO DOO DOO DOO DOO DOO DOO DOO
  DOO DOO

THEY'LL BE GA GA AT THE GO GO
WHEY THEY SEE ME IN MY TOGA

MY TOGA MADE OF BLOND
   BRILLIANTINED
BIBLICAL HAIR

MY HAIR LIKE JESUS WORE IT
HALLELUJAH I ADORE IT

HALLELUJAH MARY LOVED HER SON
WHY DON'T MY MOTHER LOVE ME

HAIR HAIR
HAIR HAIR HAIR
HAIR HAIR HAIR

FLOW IT
SHOW IT
LONG AS GOD CAN GROW IT
MY HAIR

> (*Mom ecstatically embraces the Boys, this time with warm, motherly affection. Dad shakes all their hands.*)

MOM

Oooooo, these boys love to dress up like this . . . I love them . . . I love all of you . . . I wish every mother and father would make a speech to their teen-agers: "Be free . . . no guilt . . . be whoever you are . . . do whatever you want . . . just

so you don't hurt anyone . . . I am your friend."
Can we get a picture of you?

(*Berger gives Mom his key.*)

BOYS

Sure.

MOM

Hubert!

CLAUDE

BE MANIPULATED!

ONE OF THE TRIBE

(*singing*)

I WANNA BE IN PICTURES . . .
THAT'S WHY I'M HERE, TO BE IN
PICTURES . . .

WOOF

(*in a whisper to Berger*)

See him? That's you two years from now.

BERGER

(*to Woof*)

See her? That's you one year from now.

(*to Mom, aloud*)

Love your dress, call me Thursday.

MOM

Thank you. Ready, Hubert?

(*The four guys line up for a picture—Dad uses Polaroid Swinger camera.*)

Get the best YES, dear. Don't go past it. YES!

(*Berger puts his hand on Claude's crotch as Dad focuses. Neither Dad nor Mom sees this.*)

CLAUDE

We're the Grope Group!

(*Dad snaps the picture.*)

MOM

Thank you. Thank you one and all.

(*to audience*)

I WOULD JUST LIKE TO SAY THAT IT IS
   MY CONVICTION
THAT LONGER HAIR AND OTHER
   FLAMBOYANT AFFECTATIONS
OF APPEARANCE ARE NOTHING MORE
THAN THE MALE'S EMERGENCE FROM
   HIS DRAB CAMOUFLAGE

INTO THE GAUDY PLUMAGE
WHICH IS THE BIRTHRIGHT OF HIS SEX

THERE IS A PECULIAR NOTION THAT
    ELEGANT PLUMAGE
AND FINE FEATHERS ARE NOT PROPER
    FOR THE MAN
WHEN ACTUALLY THAT IS THE WAY
    THINGS ARE
IN MOST SPECIES

> (*The Tribe hold out their hands for money.*)

Good-bye all you sweet little flowerpots.

> (*Dad and Mom exit.*)

THE TRIBE

Fuck you, Margaret Mead.

> (*As if saying, most cheerily: "Thank you, Margaret Mead."*)

HUD

Scene One: Sheila's Entrance.

CLAUDE

> (*to audience*)

Fasten your jockstraps!

BERGER

She is flying in at an altitude of 10,000 rubles.

> (*Sheila enters carrying purse, packages, cardboard posters.*)

SHEILA

Bergerbaby, I thought that was you.

WOOF

> (*He does a kazoo flourish.*)

It's Joan of Arc.

> (*He gives another kazoo toot.*)

SHEILA

SHEILA FRANKLIN
SECOND SEMESTER
NYU
AND SHE'S A PROTESTOR

> (*dropping her belongings*)

Hi, Hud.

> (*Hud runs to Sheila, kisses her entire body as she talks to audience.*)

I'll probably major in social psychology garbage. Or I might flunk out or quit. My mother and father and older sister and her husband and baby live in Portchester. I live in the East Village

with a sweet painter, Andrew . . . who moved
in after I had an affair with that one . . .

> (*She throws a daffodil at Berger, who
> raises his hand.*)

. . . and I'm much happier.

> (*breaking from embrace with Hud and
> speaking to Berger*)

Is that cool enough for you?

> (*to audience*)

I'm very social-injustice conscious.

SHE LOVES PROTESTS IN THE PARK
LIKE HE SAID: SHE'S JOAN OF ARC
VOICES AND ALL
SHEILA FRANKLIN

CLAUDE, WOOF, HUD
SHEILA FRANKLIN

SHEILA

> (*running to Woof, hugging him*)

Runaway Woof, the flower child.

WOOF

> (*as Sheila is hugging him—to Berger*)

Bananaberger, Sheila's back, baby.

HUD

Scene Two: Sheila and Berger.

BERGER

This Indian land, buzz off.

CLAUDE

When did you get in? I thought you were picketing in D.C.

BERGER

Protesting!!!

SHEILA

Spreading the groovy revolution.

WOOF

(*throws his arm around Berger's neck*)

Let's go over to the park, man, and scare some tourists.

SHEILA

(*to audience*)

Isn't love beautiful?

BERGER

Hello, Sheila.

SHEILA

Hello, Claude.

(*Note: Berger is being pleasant, genuinely, to Sheila; Sheila is the one who is resentful and refuses to say "Hello, Berger."*)

CLAUDE

Hello, Sheila.

BERGER

Hello, Sheila.

CLAUDE

Hello, Sheila.
　　　(*pause*)

SHEILA

Hello, Claude.

WOOF

Com'on, man, let's split.

SHEILA

Guess what, Claude, from President Johnson's bedroom window Eartha Kitt waved to Sheila Franklin!

BERGER

Disgrace!

CLAUDE

(*to Hud*)

Another cup of blood for

(*pointing to Sheila*)

LBJ.

SHEILA

(*looking at Berger*)

Thanks, Aquarius.

HUD

(*reading from a magazine*)

"The draft is white people sending black people to make war on yellow people to defend the land they stole from red people."

CLAUDE

We missed you, Sheila.

SHEILA

Did you really?

CLAUDE

Didn't we miss her, Berger?

BERGER

Yeah! We did.

SHEILA

(*speaks to Berger for first time, handing him poster material*)

Berger has to help Sheila make posters.

(*She returns to Claude.*)

BERGER

We're always making posters, Miss Poster. What're the posters for this time?

SHEILA

For the end of the show, stupid.

(*to Claude*)

Did Berger miss Sheila?

BERGER

Claude missed Sheila.

HUD

Tomorrow morning on the front steps at City

Hall there will be a huge suck-in for peace.
Bring your blankets and something to suck.

WOOF

What did she get you this time?

SHEILA

(*holding up yellow satin shirt to Claude*)

Sheila brought back Berger a beautiful yellow
satin shirt. Take that filthy rag off.

(*throws shirt to Berger*)

Claude, help me make these posters.

(*taking posters from Berger to Claude*)

BERGER

Oooooooooo, Sheila! My eyes cannot behold such
beauty . . .

SHEILA

(*to Berger*)

You dig, delicious?

(*Berger takes off his shirt.*)

WOOF

A body's a wonderful thing.

SHEILA

(*scratches Berger's back*)

Give me some skin, baby.

HUD

Scene Three: Sheila's Rape!

(*Claude tears holes in paper napkin, opens it, pastes it on his face as a mask.*)

BERGER

Ooooo, Sheila, you shouldn't have . . . I'm turned on, flipped out, switched on . . . you really shouldn't have done it. It's too boss, a groove, a gas. Send me to Saigon, it's the grassy end . . . it's just superlative . . .

SHEILA

Berger, stop it . . . you like it?

BERGER

(*suddenly very angry*)

Don't tell me to stop. You always do that. You don't allow me to have any friends, you're jealous, suspicious, you use the double standard, you test me, spy on me, you nag, nag, nag, you won't allow me to be myself, you follow me, you're always picking a fight, and then you expect me to

love you . . . well, I can't have sex that way . . .
sex! That's the last thing I'd want . . .

SHEILA

Berger, you're so crazy, I adore you. Please put
it on.

BERGER

It's super-goosey-gassy. I'm turny on-ey, I'm
flipey outey, stoney switchey oney, I'm freakey
outey, hungey-upey, I'm hung, I'm hung, I'm
hung, I'm hung, I'm hung, I'm hung, I'm
hung . . .

> (*During this next, he grabs Woof and has
> him get on top of Sheila, screwing her.*)

. . . head like a freaked-out Frankenstein, belt
buckle ajar, write "Fugs" on the wall, I'm buzz-
in' out on glue you, stand back banana, airplane,
rocket, pencil, smoke stack, I'm hung on the
sides, over the ears, down my leg and straight
down my back, open the door, pull it out . . .
my shirt collar . . . I'm hung . . . everybody
groove and stare . . . no underwear . . . I'm
hung . . .

> (*Berger collapses onto Woof's sleeping bag,
> as though he has just expended himself in an
> orgasm.*)

Woof, it's sex not a stomachache.

[*Note: Berger has just fucked Sheila in pub-*
lic. Or rather raped *her in public. Berger*
has had his orgasm. She was fighting him
off and reacts to his attack.]

HUD

Scene Four: Claude loves Sheila.

CLAUDE

(*removing napkin-mask from his face, as*
though nothing had happened)

Sheila, I wrote a great part for you in my movie.

SHEILA

Huh?

CLAUDE

I wrote a great part for you in my movie.

SHEILA

Huh?

CLAUDE

Yes, I did.

SHEILA

(*in shock*)

We have to make posters. We have to make posters.

(*Poster in Background: "Legalize Abortion"*)

CLAUDE

It's about a chick hung up on this straight cat . . . no it isn't . . . It's about this girl in love with this square guy . . . but she gets mixed up with somebody like Berger . . . searching for her self-identity, you know, alienated youth in a totally committed society and all that shit . . . Here . . . See: "Sheila: nineteen years old, waist-length, straight, mouse-blonde hair, unkempt, somewhat unclean, very bright, the least dressy of all the girls, but pretty underneath it all. Involved in protest marches and a student at N.Y.U."

SHEILA

Let me see that.

(*She takes script and reads.*)

"Berger? Eighteen years old, long dark hair, bright, funny, wild, but serious underneath it all. Claude's best friend. Woof! Hud!" Your movie's about us!

CLAUDE

I told you. Here, read this scene with me.

(*reading*)

"Medium long shot: Sheila and Claude entering the bar.

(*to Sheila with North Country English accent*)

"Don't you ever get lonely?"

SHEILA

"Of course I do but I don't dwell on it, do I?"

CLAUDE

"What would you like to drink?"

SHEILA

"Just coffee."

CLAUDE

"I'll have a Guinness, please. I'm sorry, Sheila. Shouldn't have been so careless . . . all my fault."

SHEILA

"I just hope I'm not knocked up. I don't want to have a baby, do I?"

CLAUDE

"I wonder if you would say the same thing if it were Berger's baby."

SHEILA

Claude, I don't understand why you're writing this about me!

CLAUDE

"You still love Berger and you're having my baby."

SHEILA

"Oh, Claude, please let's not start again. I can't take it." Oh, Claude, please with this. I really *can't* take it.

CLAUDE

(*hitting the table hard*)

"All right, I don't care what you do. Get rid of it if that's what you want."

SHEILA

Claude, excuse me, please, before I throw up. You've got a sick mind. Write a poster!

(*Claude takes his script and a poster and sits in bathtub.*

Turning to Berger)

You really like the shirt?

BERGER

Why don't you give it to Claude? It'll look better on him.

WOOF

Give it to me.

SHEILA

I'm trying to control myself, sometimes you go just too far.

BERGER

What do you want from my life? Just leave me alone.

SHEILA

Cool it, baby. Groove on a poster.

BERGER

Sheila.

SHEILA

Creative time! I didn't know I could still get to you.

BERGER

Sheila, who's gonna leave? You or me?

SHEILA

Why're you so up-tight, groovy?

WOOF

(*to Claude*)

He got kicked out of school.

CLAUDE

What?

BERGER

Woof!

WOOF

He got kicked out of school!

SHEILA

What do you mean . . . he got . . . he got . . .

BERGER

Burn the schools to the ground, men. Graffiti the blackboards.

SHEILA

When did it happen . . . this is terrible.

BERGER

This morning morning and it's a groovy day. I switch off, move me to Suburbia. I surrender, carpet me wall to wall.

(*to Claude, climbing into bathtub*)

Move over. I'm Vietnam bait, Claudio.

WOOF

If I hear this Vietnam one more time, I'm leaving this theater.

SHEILA

He got kicked out?

CLAUDE

High School Drop-Outs should drop dead.

SHEILA

Wait a minute . . . wait a minute.

WOOF

Sheila, do you know any groovy miniskirts?

SHEILA

Shut up, Quasimodo!

BERGER

Don't get your balls in an uproar, Sheila. School never did anything for my Twentieth-Century computer.

CLAUDE

Shit, I'm a patriot, but I'm a patriot for the whole damn world.

BERGER

Education squashes my growth.

CLAUDE

I'm not going to die for my country.

SHEILA

Well, then, die for something else.

CLAUDE

I'd rather live and rot in jail a few years.

SHEILA

Claude, tell them you don't want to kill people. Tell them you're against killing people.

CLAUDE

Oh, that this too too solid flesh would melt.

BERGER

Back to Miss Poster's posters.

WOOF

Let's blow, Berg.

SHEILA

He's irresponsible. He's insensitive. He lies.

BERGER

Let's blow our minds on these, Toulouse.

SHEILA

He's neurotic, he's a pothead. Let the stupid Army get him.

CLAUDE

Let the stupid Army get *him?* What about me?

SHEILA

He's an uncommitted, hedonistic jerk.

BERGER

How many do we need, Miss N.Y.U.?

SHEILA

He's paranoid.

BERGER

I thought we saved the signs from before.

CLAUDE

Sheila, how about a flick tonight or something, and we can really talk about Berger.

BERGER

What should I say?

SHEILA

Talk about Berger in a movie?

CLAUDE

Come to the movies with me, Sheila.

SHEILA

I've got a date with the park police.

BERGER

What do you dig in that Death Body, Sheila, man? She puts you down bad.

CLAUDE

What does she dig in your Death Body, man?

BERGER

Whatever it is, I'd like to chop it off.

SHEILA

I had plans for you.

BERGER

Sheila, be a good fly, buzz off.

(*Hud enters with Dionne, bringing two cups of coffee.*)

HUD

Blood for Sheila, Watusi Katanga.

SHEILA

I gotta split.

BERGER

Drink it and come together.

SHEILA

(*to Berger*)

You and me.

CLAUDE

(*to Sheila*)

You and me.

WOOF

(*to Berger*)

You and me.

HUD

(*to Dionne*)

Walla walla. Gooba gooba.

BERGER

Do you know what Sheila, the Sex Swamp, likes to do in bed? She loves to . . .

HUD

Miobie Manatoga.

SHEILA

Berg, oh, George Berger . . . I just want to be
your friend . . .

HUD

Walla walla . . . voodoo waba . . .

DIONNE

Stop that, Hud . . . stop putting us down all the
time, Bwana bwana.

BERGER

We're finished . . . we've had it . . . I don't see
you anymore.

SHEILA

You're like everything you're against.

BERGER

I never did see you.

HUD

Boogie Woogie.

DIONNE

Don't talk that way.

SHEILA

You talk about freedom . . .

BERGER

I'm off limits to you.

CLAUDE

Let's go see "Whips and Satin" on Forty-second Street.

HUD

Bad scene. Bad scene.

SHEILA

Don't put up a wall.

CLAUDE

Come to the flicks.

BERGER

Forbidden. This way out.

SHEILA

No bicycling. No skating. No littering. No loitering. No spitting. No smoking. No eating. No tipping. No talking. No singing. No browsing. No breathing. No loving.

DEAD END
DONT WALK
KEEP OUT
RED LIGHT
RED LIGHT

STEEP CLIFF
BEWARE
MAD DOG
BLIND MAN
BLIND MAN

WARNING LAND MINE
HIGH VOLTAGE LINE
DONT MAKE A PASS
KEEP OFF THE GRASS

DETOUR
WET PAINT
HANDS OFF
DEAD END
DEAD END

SHARP CURVE
STEEP HILL
DANGER
ONE-WAY
ONE-WAY

EMER-
GENCY
EXIT
ONLY
ONLY

WARNING MARKERS HIDDEN
LOITERING FORBIDDEN
ALL TRESPASSERS WILL BE SHOT
CLAUDE LOVES SHEILA—HE BETTER
   LOVE HER NOT

WET PAINT
HANDS OFF
KEEP OUT
DEAD END
DEAD END

SHEILA	ALL
DEAD END	DEAD END
DON'T WALK	
KEEP OUT	
RED LIGHT	KEEP OUT
RED LIGHT	KEEP OUT
STEEP CLIFF	STOP SIGN
BEWARE	
MAD DOG	
BLIND MAN	TURN OFF
BLIND MAN	TURN OFF

WARNING·LAND MINE
HIGH VOLTAGE LINE
DONT MAKE A PASS
KEEP OFF THE GRASS

DETOUR   DETOUR
WET PAINT
HANDS OFF
DEAD END   DO NOT
DEAD END   ENTER

SHARP CURVE   NO TURNS
STEEP HILL
DANGER
ONE-WAY   DEAD END
ONE-WAY   DEAD END

EMER-   KEEP OUT
GENCY
EXIT
ONLY   WET PAINT
ONLY   BLIND MAN

WARNING MARKERS HIDDEN
LOITERING FORBIDDEN
ALL TRESPASSERS WILL BE SHOT
CLAUDE LOVES SHEILA—
    HE BETTER LOVE HER NOT

WET PAINT	HANDS OFF
HANDS OFF	
KEEP OUT	
DEAD END	DEAD END
DEAD END	DEAD END
	MEN WORKING
DEAD END	
	MEN WORKING
DEAD END	
	NO STANDING
DEAD END	
	NO PARKING
DEAD END	
	NO SMOKING
DEAD END	
	NO JOKING
DEAD END	
DEAD END	
MY FRIEND	

(Blackout. Lights up on Berger and Woof with an old, battle-torn American flag)

WOOF *and* BERGER

(both high)

Om mane padme om

THIS IS THE DAWNING OF THE AGE OF AQUARIUS

James Rado as CLAUDE   HELLO, I'M A HUMAN BEING

Gerome Ragni as BERGER   WHAT IS IT—A BOY OR A GIRL?

FOUR SCORE AND SEVEN YEARS AGO...

I GOT LIFE!

I'M HUNG

HAIR!!!

HAPPY BIRTHDAY, ABIE BABY!

FATHER,
WHY DO THESE
WORDS SOUND
SO NASTY?

WHITE BOYS GIVE ME GOOSE BUMPS

OH—THE BED!

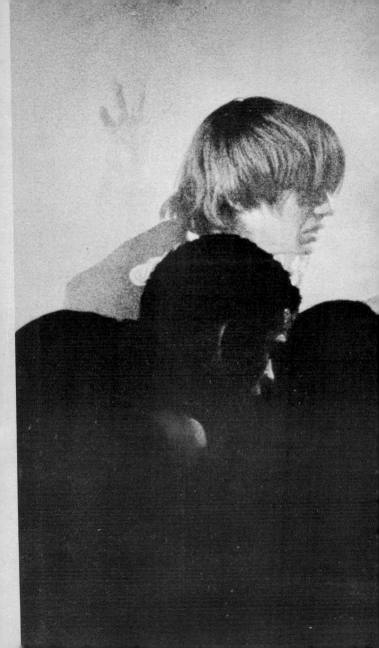

CRAZY FOR THE RED WHITE AND BLUE AND YELLOW...FRINGE

BEADS, FLOWERS, FREEDOM, HAPPINESS

PEACE NOW! FREEDOM NOW!

WHAT A PIECE OF WORK IS MAN

Om mane padme om
Om mane padme om
Shanti Shanti Shanti

WOOF

Folding the flag means taking care of the nation.
Folding the flag means putting it to bed for the
    night.
I fell through a hole in the flag.
I got lost in the folds of the flag.

WOOF *and* BERGER

DON'T PUT IT DOWN
BEST ONE AROUND
CRAZY FOR THE RED BLUE AND WHITE
CRAZY FOR THE RED BLUE AND WHITE

YOU LOOK AT ME
WHAT DO YOU SEE
CRAZY FOR THE WHITE RED AND BLUE
CRAZY FOR THE WHITE RED AND BLUE

CAUSE I LOOK DIFFERENT
YOU THINK I'M SUBVERSIVE
CRAZY FOR THE BLUE WHITE AND RED
CRAZY FOR THE BLUE WHITE AND RED

MY HEART BEATS TRUE
FOR THE RED WHITE AND BLUE
CRAZY FOR THE BLUE WHITE AND RED
CRAZY FOR THE BLUE WHITE AND RED
  AND YELLOW FRINGE

CRAZY FOR THE BLUE WHITE RED
  AND YELLOW

BERGER

Com'on watch us burn it at the Be-In!

> (*Berger and Woof exit. Claude stands next to lowered Waverly Theater marquee. Mom, carrying stool, speaking as she enters*)

MOM IN BOX-OFFICE

Waverly Theater . . . The Assassination and Hallucination of the Marat de Sade directed by the Inmates of the Asylum of Charenton starring Peter Brook at 8:15 and 11:10 together with the Gorilla Queen performed live by the Judson Memorial Church at ten o'clock. This is a recording and thanks for calling the Waverly.

> (*hangs up—to Claude*)

Move on, you. You can't stand here if you don't buy a ticket.

CLAUDE

(to audience)

THE FLESH FAILURES

WE STARVE-LOOK AT ONE ANOTHER
   SHORT OF BREATH
WALKING PROUDLY IN OUR WINTER
   COATS
WEARING SMELLS FROM
   LABORATORIES
FACING A DYING NATION OF MOVING
   PAPER FANTASY
LISTENING FOR THE NEW TOLD LIES
WITH SUPREME VISIONS OF LONELY
   TUNES

SOMEWHERE INSIDE SOMETHING THERE
   IS A RUSH OF GREATNESS
WHO KNOWS WHAT STANDS IN FRONT
   OF OUR LIVES

I FASHION MY FUTURE ON FILMS IN
   SPACE
SILENCE TELLS ME SECRETLY . . .
   EVERYTHING

SINGING MY SPACE SONGS ON A
   SPIDER WEB SITAR

LIFE IS AROUND YOU AND IN YOU
ANSWER FOR TIMOTHY LEARY DEARIE

LET THE SUNSHINE IN

    (*pause*)

MOM

How many, please?

CLAUDE

I'm waiting for Sheila.

    (*Jeanie and Crissy enter. Jeanie is in her sari, Crissy in her Be-In outfit.*)

JEANIE

Let the beatniks through, please. Excuse me, sir, did you see a mooky-lookin' blond guy *cruisin'* around here?

CLAUDE

Hi, Jeanie.

JEANIE

Why didn't you call me?

CLAUDE

I been busy looking for a job.

JEANIE

What's the matter, you embarrassed? We had a good time, didn't we?

CLAUDE

I had to take my physical for the Army.

JEANIE

What are you doing here? Waiting for somebody?

CLAUDE

No, no, I'm going to the movies.

MOM

How many, please? The feature's about to begin.

JEANIE

Want some company? I've got my own bread.

CLAUDE

No, I'm meeting Berger.

JEANIE

Like my new button? Psychedelicize South Korea.

MOM

Move on, you! You can't stand here if you don't buy a ticket.

CLAUDE

I gotta go.

MOM

How many, please?

CLAUDE

Just one.

JEANIE

Claude, I just saw Sheila. She can't make it. She won't be able to meet you. She'll be at the Be-In if you want to see her.

CLAUDE

I'd like a refund, please.

MOM

(*now very sweet*)

Sorry, we don't give refunds.

CLAUDE

But I changed my mind, Rosie. I just bought the ticket.

MOM

Sorry, we have our rules.

CLAUDE

I already saw this film.

MOM

You'll have to see the manager.

CLAUDE

(*to Mom*)

Forget it!

JEANIE

Come with the beatniks to the Be-In, Claude.

CLAUDE

Forget it . . . I'm going to the movies. Tell Sheila you didn't see me.

JEANIE

Watch the FAGS don't get you.

CLAUDE

Drop dead.

(*exits*)

JEANIE

He loves me.

(*The Tribe enter through the audience and pass out leaflets announcing the Be-In simultaneous with Jeanie's speech.*)

Dig it, people, I'm tripped, high, zonked, stoned, right here, right now in this theater. I've had every drug going except some jungle vines somewhere. I have a right to put anything I want in my body. What's going on inside all those little Daily News heads? Anybody who says Pot is bad is full of shit. This is my living room and I'm gonna say something I always wanted to say, "Alan Burke Sucks."

THE TRIBE

Come to the Be-In. See the Hippies get busted by the New York City Police. See them smoke Marijuana, the killer weed. Bring your own Pot. Tourists . . . See the Hippies. See the land of the Underground Movies. See the freak show. See them . . . The gypsy tribes . . . Watch the beatniks . . . See them get arrested . . . See the

Potheads get busted by the Federal Bureau of Narcotics. See . . . see the Hippie Phenomenon.

JEANIE

(*to Crissy*)

Well, are you going to stay here, or are you going to the Be-In like a human being?

CRISSY

I'm gonna wait.

JEANIE

You've got no face, Crissy, no face.

CRISSY

I MET A BOY CALLED FRANK MILLS
ON SEPTEMBER TWELFTH RIGHT HERE
   IN FRONT OF THE WAVERLY
BUT UNFORTUNATELY I LOST HIS
   ADDRESS

HE WAS LAST SEEN WITH HIS FRIEND,
   A DRUMMER
HE RESEMBLED GEORGE HARRISON OF
   THE BEATLES
BUT HE WEARS HIS HAIR TIED IN A
   SMALL BOW AT THE BACK

I LOVE HIM
BUT IT EMBARRASSES ME TO WALK
   DOWN THE STREET WITH HIM
HE LIVES IN BROOKLYN SOMEWHERE
AND WEARS THIS WHITE CRASH
   HELMET

HE HAS GOLD CHAINS ON HIS
   LEATHER JACKET
AND ON THE BACK IS WRITTEN THE
   NAMES
MARY AND MOM AND HELL'S ANGELS

I WOULD GRATEFULLY APPRECIATE IT
IF YOU SEE HIM TELL HIM I'M IN THE
   PARK WITH MY GIRL FRIEND
AND PLEASE

TELL HIM ANGELA AND I
DON'T WANT THE TWO DOLLARS
   BACK . . .
JUST HIM

> (*The Be-In . . . The sound of bells from offstage, from the back of the theater, from the aisles. Ankle, wrist, hand bells. The Tribe enter from all directions with their bells, carrying candles and incense, enveloping the audience, first with the slight, in-*

*sistent rhythm, moving into "Hare Krishna,"
the rhythms building throughout the scene.
A peace-pipe is passed around. Flowers,
fruit and raisins, and nuts, given out. Flowers and incense to the audience.*

*Dad and Mom begin their participation in
the scene at its outskirts, employing their
rational, establishment, middle-class view-
points and logic against the music of the
Be-In—the music which never ceases.)*

THE TRIBE

HARE KRISHNA HARE KRISHNA
KRISHNA KRISHNA HARE HARE

HARE RAMA HARE RAMA
RAMA RAMA HARE HARE

*(This repeats several times, as kids envelop
the stage, and under it comes the chant)*

LOVE LOVE
LOVE LOVE
LOVE LOVE
LOVE LOVE

DROP OUT
DROP OUT
DROP OUT
DROP OUT

BE IN
BE IN
BE IN
BE IN

HARE KRISHNA HARE KRISHNA
KRISHNA KRISHNA HARE HARE

HARE RAMA HARE RAMA
RAMA RAMA HARE HARE

BEADS FLOWERS FREEDOM HAPPINESS
BEADS FLOWERS FREEDOM HAPPINESS
BEADS FLOWERS FREEDOM HAPPINESS
BEADS FLOWERS FREEDOM HAPPINESS

SMOKE SMOKE SMOKE
SMOKE SMOKE SMOKE
TAKE TRIPS
GET HIGH
LAUGH JOKE AND GOOD-BYE

BEAT DRUM AND OLD TIN POT
I'M HIGH ON YOU KNOW WHAT

BEAT DRUM AND OLD TIN POT
I'M HIGH ON YOU KNOW WHAT

HIGH HIGH HIGH HIGH
WAY WAY UP HERE
IONOSPHERE

LOVE LOVE LOVE LOVE LOVE
LOVE LOVE LOVE LOVE LOVE

HARE KRISHNA HARE KRISHNA
KRISHNA KRISHNA HARE HARE

HARE RAMA HARE RAMA
RAMA RAMA HARE RAMA

LOVE LOVE LOVE LOVE
LOVE LOVE LOVE LOVE
LOVE SEX LOVE SEX
LOVE SEX LOVE SEX

HARE KRISHNA HARE KRISHNA
KRISHNA KRISHNA HARE HARE
ETC.
ETC.

MOM

We had another generation before you who
went to war, went to colleges, worked for a
salary . . . you're a disgrace to this country . . .

you are certainly mixed up, all of you . . . just bringing attention to yourselves.

ANNOUNCER-MAN

(neutral, religious, manly)

Keep America strong.
Make America stronger.
May God bring our nation victory.

DAD

We're fighting a war. Use atomic weapons and win it, for Crissake. Get China now, before they get us, and have faith in God and Nation and the Military-Industrial Complex.

ANNOUNCER-FEMALE

(factual, unemotional, matter-of-fact)

A demonstration to end United States involvement in Vietnam will be held on Saturday at one P.M. We're going to meet at Times Square and march around the world.

MOM

Oh, you're all so naïve about the power structure of our civilization. The subtleties, the intricacies, the complexities . . . you don't know what's really going on . . . the *top secret truth* about what's really happening in Red China.

ANNOUNCER-MAN

(*unctuously*)

The LSD Research Group sponsors a series of psychedelic lectures and celebrations on various aspects of the effect of LSD—"The Death of the Mind." How should you give a person LSD? Who regards LSD as dangerous? Tickets five dollars at the door. Or by appointment in advance. At the Planetarium Subway Station. Or call PO 3-3333-3333.

DAD

You parents should care more about *sex* and stop worrying about the drugs. Drugs are innocent compared to the violence mixed up with *sex*. Did you realize this? It is time to deal with this sex mess. Sex isn't love or even pleasure anymore . . . They preach love . . . narcotic love.

MOM

What does a nineteen-year-old kid know?

THE TRIBE

MARI JUANA MARI JUANA
JUANA JUANA MARI MARI

MARI JUANA MARI JUANA
JUANA JUANA MARI MARI

> (*The Tribe respond to Dad and Mom's invectives only with more song, stronger rhythm, and by bedecking Dad and Mom with flowers, beads, loading their arms with gifts, fruit, etc.*)

MOM

You kids don't appreciate the maturity and wisdom that age brings.

> (*to audience*)

My son wears a black arm band . . . he's an anti-war with an arm band. His father can't even walk down the street.

DAD

> (*almost to himself*)

My son doesn't like me. He doesn't like me.

MOM

We have got to help these young people. How did they get off the track? This is serious, lady.

DAD

I can't even go into my son's room. My son has no shame. He leaves everything right out in the open where I can see it.

MOM

He is our son, dear, and we are his mummy and daddy.

(*Dad and Mom as a result become more incensed, enraged, angry, moving closer and closer to the center of the Be-In all the while.*)

DAD

(*now walking among The Tribe, looking around at them and getting very upset*)

What's happening to our bedrock foundation of baths and underarm deodorant? How do they eat? Where do they sleep? Why do they have to be dressed like this?

MOM

(*walking among The Tribe*)

Flower power, putting on, turning on, blowing the mind . . . what language do you speak?

DAD

In two months my son will be in Vietnam and is going to be killed, and I'm proud of him.

MOM

Physical contact with any of these animals would repulse me.

(*to audience*)

I say, support our fighting, short-haired men in Vietnam.

DAD

(*intensely frustrated at not being able to penetrate The Tribe's concern with the Be-In, and shouting*)

I'd like to see one of your Daffodil Crowd in front of a machine gun.

MOM

(*shouting above their chants*)

Ship these Peaceniks to the Vietnam meat-grinder.

THE TRIBE

HARE KRISHNA HARE KRISHNA
KRISHNA KRISHNA HARE HARE

HARE RAMA HARE RAMA
RAMA RAMA HARE HARE

>*(This chant continues as a new chant de-*
>*velops behind it and overtakes it.)*

STRIP
STRIP
STRIP
STRIP
STRIP
STRIP
STRIP
STRIP STRIP
STRIP STRIP
STRIP STRIP
STRIP STRIP
STRIP STRIP STRIP
STRIP STRIP STRIP
STRIP STRIP STRIP
STRIP STRIP STRIP
STRIP STRIP STRIP
STRIP STRIP STRIP

>*(This chant predominates now with the*
>*ferocious intensity of the drums. Berger has*
>*removed all his clothes by this time and is*
>*seen totally naked for a brief moment by*
>*the audience. He is then surrounded by The*
>*Tribe, but the Police-Puppets have seen him*
>*and close in for an arrest. The Tribe form*

a protective wall against the Police and
sing)

THE TRIBE

WE LOVE COPS
WE LOVE COPS
WE LOVE COPS
WE LOVE COPS

HARE KRISHNA   WE LOVE COPS
  HARE KRISHNA   WE LOVE COPS
KRISHNA KRISHNA   WE LOVE COPS
  HARE HARE   WE LOVE COPS
                      WE LOVE COPS

HARE RAMA
  HARE RAMA
RAMA RAMA
  HARE HARE

(*A large flag is held aloft on two poles. It*
dates from about 1776. It has a green pine
tree in its center on a yellow field. A rattle-
snake twines about the tree trunk. Be-
low it reads: "Don't Tread on Me." Above
the tree it reads: "An Appeal to Heaven."

Violent drumming on oil drums, as Sheila
comes forward holding a flaming Maxwell
House coffee can in her right hand above

(*her head. She strikes a Statue of Liberty pose.*)

THE TRIBE

Democracy's Daughter!

(*In her other hand, Sheila holds a bunch of daffodils. One by one, each guy comes forward, lighting their draft cards, dropping the remains into the can. As each card is burned, The Tribe cheers. Sheila gives each guy a daffodil in exchange. Claude is last; he approaches the can, hesitates a moment, holds his card above it, it catches fire and he pulls it back quickly, extinguishing the flame.*

Sheila puts the flaming can center stage; The Tribe sits around it, as if it were their campfire, huddling in blankets, as the drums die away rapidly.

Claude stands apart and sings)

CLAUDE

WHERE DO I GO
FOLLOW THE RIVER
WHERE DO I GO
FOLLOW THE GULLS

WHERE IS THE SOMETHING
WHERE IS THE SOMEONE
THAT TELLS ME WHY
I LIVE AND DIE

WHERE DO I GO
FOLLOW THE CHILDREN
WHERE DO I GO
FOLLOW THEIR SMILES

IS THERE AN ANSWER
IN THEIR SWEET FACES
THAT TELLS ME WHY
I LIVE AND DIE

FOLLOW THE WIND SONG
FOLLOW THE THUNDER
FOLLOW THE LIGHTNING IN
YOUNG LOVERS' EYES

DOWN TO THE GUTTER
UP TO THE GLITTER
INTO THE CITY WHERE THE
TRUTH LIES

WHERE DO I GO
FOLLOW MY HEARTBEAT
WHERE DO I GO
FOLLOW MY HAND

WHERE WILL THEY LEAD ME
AND WILL I EVER
DISCOVER WHY
I LIVE AND DIE

THE TRIBE

WHERE DO I GO
FOLLOW THE CHILDREN
WHERE DO I GO
FOLLOW THEIR SMILES

IS THERE AN ANSWER
IN THEIR SWEET FACES
THAT TELLS ME WHY
I LIVE AND DIE

FOLLOW THE WIND SONG
FOLLOW THE THUNDER
FOLLOW THE LIGHTNING IN
YOUNG LOVERS' EYES

DOWN TO THE GUTTER
UP TO THE GLITTER
INTO THE CITY WHERE THE
TRUTH LIES

CLAUDE

WHERE DO I GO
FOLLOW MY HEARTBEAT

WHERE DO I GO
FOLLOW MY HAND

WHERE WILL THEY LEAD ME
AND WILL I EVER
DISCOVER WHY
I LIVE AND DIE

THE TRIBE

WHY

CLAUDE

I LIVE AND DIE

THE TRIBE

WHY

CLAUDE

I LIVE AND DIE

Note: At the end of the intermission, just
before Act II begins, Crissy puts two
old seventy-eight-rpm records on an antique
windup victrola. The songs: "Anything
Goes," followed by "White Cliffs of Dover";
this going into "Electric Blues."

ACT II

Band on stage now. This is the Intergalactic Bathtub electrified. Moving light projections.

The sound from the band is full and furious. The band is The Leather Bag—four guys dressed in leather outfits—perhaps black, brown, and white in color. Electric wiring everywhere, from amplifiers, guitars, hand mikes, and even from the leather costumes —wires from backs, heads, fingers, hands, feet, crotches.

The Tribe dances.

Note: All the kids wear military uniforms, mismatching, etc.

THE LEATHER BAG

WE'RE ALL ENCASED IN SONIC ARMOR

BELTIN' IT OUT THROUGH CHROME
   GRENADES
MILES AND MILES OF MEDUSAN CHORD
THE ELECTRONIC SONIC BOOM

IT'S WHAT'S HAPPENING BABY
IT'S WHERE IT'S AT DADDY

THEY CHAIN YA AND BRAINWASH YA
WHEN YOU LEAST SUSPECT IT
THEY FEED YA MASS MEDIA
THE AGE IS ELECTRIC

I GOT THE ELECTRIC BLUES
I GOT THE ELECTRIC BLUES
I GOT THE ELECTRIC BLUES
I GOT THE ELECTRIC BLUES

THWUMP . . .   OLD
   RACKETY . . .   FASHION
   WHOMP   MELODY
ROCK . . . FOLK ROCK . . .
   RHYTHM AND BLUES
ELECTRONS   OLD
   EXPLODIN' . . .   FASHION
   RACKETY-CLACK   MELODY
THWUMP . . . WHOOMP . . .
   WHUMP

PLUGGED IN . . .   OLD
   TURNED ON   FASHION
RACKETY . . . SHOMP . . .   MELODY
   ROCK
ROCK . . . FOLK ROCK . . .
   RHYTHM AND BLUES
THWUMP . . .
   RACKETY-CLACK
WHOOMP . . . WHUMP . . .
   POOF
CAVED IN . . . CAVED IN
   . . . YES CAVED IN

LYRICS SHATTER LIKE BROKEN GLASS
IN THE SONIC BOOM
LYRICS SHATTER LIKE BROKEN GLASS
ELECTRONIC DOOM

I GOT THE ELECTRIC BLUES
I GOT THE ELECTRIC BLUES
I GOT THE ELECTRIC BLUES
I GOT THE ELECTRIC BLUES

    (The tempo slows, the music softens.)

TELL ME WHO DO YOU LOVE MAN?
TELL ME WHAT MAN?
TELL ME WHAT'S IT YOU LOVE MAN?

AN OLD FASHION MELODY

TELL ME WHAT'S IT THAT MOVES YOU?
TELL ME WHAT'S IT THAT
  GROOVES YOU?

AN OLD FASHION MELODY

BUT OLD SONGS LEAVE YOU DEAD
WE SELL OUR SOULS FOR BREAD

  (*back to the beat and the fury*)

WE'RE ALL ENCASED IN SONIC ARMOR
BELTIN' IT OUT THROUGH CHROME
  GRENADES
MILES AND MILES OF MEDUSAN CHORD
THE ELECTRONIC SONIC BOOM

IT'S WHAT'S HAPPENING BABY
IT'S WHERE IT'S AT DADDY

THEY CHAIN YA AND BRAINWASH YA
WHEN YOU LEAST SUSPECT IT
THEY FEED YA MASS MEDIA
THE AGE IS ELECTRIC

I GOT THE ELECTRIC BLUES
I GOT THE ELECTRIC BLUES
I GOT THE ELECTRIC BLUES
I GOT THE ELECTRIC BLUES

THWUMP . . . RACKETY . . .　　OLD
　　WHOMP　　　　　　　　　　FASHION
ROCK . . . FOLK ROCK . . .　　MELODY
　　RHYTHM AND BLUES
ELECTRONICS　　　　　　　　　OLD
　　EXPLODIN' . . .　　　　　　FASHION
　　RACKETY-CLACK　　　　　　MELODY
THWUMP . . . WHOOMP . .
　　WHUMP
PLUGGED IN . . .　　　　　　　OLD
　　TURNED ON　　　　　　　　FASHION
RACKETY . . . SHOOMP . . .　　MELODY
　　ROCK
ROCK . . . FOLK ROCK . . .
　　RHYTHM AND BLUES
THWUMP . . .
　　RACKETY-CLACK
WHOOMP. . . WHUMP . . .
　　POOF
CAVED IN . . . CAVED IN
　　. . . YES CAVED IN

LYRICS SHATTER　　　　(*shouting*)
　　LIKE
　　BROKEN GLASS　　AMPLIFIERS HIGHER
IN THE SONIC　　　　　TURN 'EM UP HIGHER
　　BOOM　　　　　　　AMPLIFIERS HIGHER
LYRICS SHATTER　　　　TURN 'EM UP HIGHER
　　　　　　　　　　　　HIGHER HIGHER

LIKE LOUDER LOUDER
BROKEN GLASS FIRE FIRE
ELECTRONIC
DOOM

*(The amplifiers, the mikes, the power sys-
tems explode, but The Leather Bag go on
singing and playing, no sound coming out,
The Tribe continue dancing to no music
The words are mouthed.)*

I GOT THE
ELECTRIC BLUES
I GOT THE
ELECTRIC BLUES
I GOT THE
ELECTRIC BLUES
I GOT THE
ELECTRIC BLUES

*(The Tribe dance,
screaming out every
time The Leather Bag
sing "I got the Elec-
tric Blues.")*

*(The Tribe clear the dance floor, leaving
Sheila and Berger dancing to a soft snare
from the drummer. They dance awhile before speaking.)*

BERGER

*(speaking and singing as they dance; to
audience)*

Claude Hooper Bukowski leaves us tomorrow
morning.

SHEILA

(*to Berger*)

I *like* Claude. But that's as far as I can take it.

BERGER

Claude has been drafted.

SHEILA

Claude's going to play soldier.

BERGER

(*to audience*)

Tonight is for him. Sheila's gonna do Claude a favor tonight.

SHEILA

Oh, no I'm not.

BERGER

(*to audience*)

The greatest going-away gift we can give our friend.

SHEILA

What am I, the tribal sacrifice?

(*A group starts singing with the band in the background. Sheila and Berger dance throughout.*)

GROUP

HOW CAN PEOPLE BE SO HEARTLESS
HOW CAN PEOPLE BE SO CRUEL

BERGER

Sheila, you have to do this for Claude.

GROUP

EASY TO BE HARD
EASY TO BE COLD

SHEILA

Do *this? This* is a four-letter word.

GROUP

HOW CAN PEOPLE HAVE NO FEELINGS

BERGER

Please.

(*tries to kiss her*)

GROUP

HOW CAN THEY IGNORE THEIR FRIENDS

BERGER

I'll be good to you.

(*tries to embrace her*)

GROUP

EASY TO BE PROUD

SHEILA

(*breaking away from Berger*)

No!

GROUP

EASY TO SAY NO

BERGER

(*backed by the Group*)

ESPECIALLY PEOPLE WHO CARE
ABOUT STRANGERS
WHO CARE ABOUT EVIL AND
SOCIAL INJUSTICE
DO YOU ONLY CARE ABOUT
THE BLEEDING CROWD
HOW ABOUT A NEEDING FRIEND

SHEILA *and* GROUP

HOW CAN PEOPLE BE SO HEARTLESS
HOW CAN PEOPLE BE SO CRUEL

GROUP

EASY TO GIVE IN
EASY TO HELP OUT

HOW CAN PEOPLE HAVE NO FEELINGS
YOU KNOW I'M HUNG UP ON YOU

BERGER

I'll make a deal with you.

SHEILA

Sheila's the faithful kind.

BERGER

You do it tonight with Claude; I'll do it tomorrow night with you.

SHEILA

A Berger barter!

BERGER

Sheila, we got this big going-away scene planned

for Claude. If you do this for Claude, it'll make it perfect. He loves you, love.

SHEILA

Claude is a boy for going. It takes a man to say no.

BERGER

O.K., Sheila. That's it. We're finished, it's over, we've had it.

(*Berger starts walking off angrily.*)

GROUP

EASY TO BE HARD
EASY TO BE COLD
EASY TO BE PROUD
EASY TO SAY NO

(*Berger exits.*)

SHEILA

So long, love.

(*Claude enters, Sheila exits. The Tribe greet Claude with wild enthusiasm. Claude wears a white, floor-length Indian linen gown, gold-embroidered. He carries a small over-night bag and throws up into the air various gifts he has brought for The Tribe: some*

colored shirts, a Buddha, necklaces, etc.,
all of them his personal belongings.)

HUD

It's Lord Buckingham!

CLAUDE

MANCHESTER ENGLAND ENGLAND
ACROSS THE ATLANTIC SEA
AND I'M A GENIUS GENIUS
I BELIEVE IN GAWD
AND I BELIEVE THAT GAWD
    BELIEVES IN CLAUDE
THAT'S ME THAT'S ME

(*The Tribe dances around Claude singing
"Too much, too much" softly behind the
next dialogue.*)

HUD	THE TRIBE
Claude, baby, how ya' doin', man?	TOO MUCH TOO MUCH TOO MUCH TOO MUCH SUPER GOOSEY GASEY
CLAUDE	SUPER GOOSEY GASEY
I'm cooling it, ding dong.	TOO MUCH TOO MUCH TOO MUCH TOO MUCH ETC.

HUD

This is your night.

JEANIE

Oh, poor baby.

WOOF

Claude, I'm disappointed in you. I thought you said they wouldn't get you.

YOUNG MAN

You chickened out.

CLAUDE

Yeah, I'm chickenshit.

WOOF

Ah, you should've burned it and got your picture in the papers.

CLAUDE

I'm no hero . . . starting right now.

JEANIE

Claude, *that sari*, where did you get *that sari!* Barney's Boys' Town?

CLAUDE

Where's Berger?

YOUNG MAN

Clip, clip, clip . . . tomorrow morning.

(*pantomiming cutting Claude's hair*)

WOOF

Oh, leave the poor soldier boy alone.

CLAUDE

It's bad enough without you gays bugging me.

(*Dionne on bandstand with two other Negro girls. She signals to the band.*)

DIONNE

Fellas, oh, fellas!

(*The band plays a fanfare and the three girls turn to face the audience. They impersonate the Supremes. One wears a high-fashion blonde wig; all in high heels and sexy-cheap sequin dresses.*)

I want you to meet PFC Booo-Booo-Boookowski.

DIONNE *and* TWO GIRLS

(playing with Claude)

WHITE BOYS ARE SO PRETTY
SKIN AS SMOOTH AS MILK
WHITE BOYS ARE SO PRETTY
HAIR LIKE CHINESE SILK

WHITE BOYS GIVE ME GOOSE BUMPS
WHITE BOYS GIVE ME CHILLS
WHEN THEY TOUCH MY SHOULDER
THAT'S THE TOUCH THAT KILLS

MY MOTHER CALLS 'EM LILIES
I CALL 'EM PICCADILLIES
MY DADDY WARNS ME STAY AWAY
I SAY COME ON OUT AND PLAY

WHITE BOYS ARE SO GROOVY
WHITE BOYS ARE SO TOUGH
EVERY TIME THEY'RE NEAR ME
JUST CAN'T GET ENOUGH

WHITE, WHITE, WHITE, WHITE, WHITE,
  WHITE, WHITE, WHITE
WHITE BOYS

*(Jeanie pins large button on Claude's lapel:
"Support Our Boys in Vietnam.")*

WHITE BOYS ARE SO PRETTY
WHITE BOYS ARE SO SWEET
WHITE BOYS DRIVE ME CRAZY
DRIVE ME INDISCREET

(*Claude dances.*)

WHITE BOYS ARE SO SEXY
LEGS SO LONG AND LEAN
LOVE THOSE SPRAYED-ON TROUSERS
LOVE THE LOVE MACHINE

MY BROTHER CALLS 'EM RUBBLE
THEY'RE MY KIND OF TROUBLE
MY DADDY WARNS ME "NO NO NO"
BUT I SAY "WHITE BOYS GO GO GO"

(*Hud joins Claude dancing.*)

WHITE BOYS ARE SO LOVELY
BEAUTIFUL AS GIRLS
LOVE TO RUN MY FINGERS
AND TOES THRU ALL THEIR CURLS
WHITE WHITE WHITE WHITE WHITE
   WHITE WHITE WHITE
WHITE BOYS

(*Hud takes over dancing as Jeanie, Crissy, and Angela sing to him.*)

JEANIE, CRISSY, ANGELA

BLACK BOYS ARE DELICIOUS
CHOCOLATE-FLAVORED LOVE

LICORICE LIPS LIKE CANDY
KEEP MY COCOA HANDY

I HAVE SUCH A SWEET TOOTH
WHEN IT COMES TO LOVE

ONCE I TRIED A DIET
OF QUIET, REST, NO SWEETS

BUT I WENT NEARLY CRAZY
AND I WENT CLEARLY CRAZY

BECAUSE I REALLY CRAVED FOR
MY CHOCOLATE-FLAVORED TREATS

BLACK BOYS ARE NUTRITIOUS
BLACK BOYS FILL ME UP

BLACK BOYS ARE SO DAMN YUMMY
THEY SATISFY MY TUMMY

I HAVE SUCH A SWEET TOOTH
WHEN IT COMES TO LOVE
BLACK BLACK BLACK BLACK BLACK
BLACK BLACK BLACK
BLACK BOYS

(joined by Dionne's trio)

WHITE BOYS
BLACK BOYS
WHITE BOYS
BLACK BOYS

MIXED MEDIA . . .

CLAUDE

Hey, Woof, from my bedroom to your bedroom.

(hands Woof rolled-up photo)

WOOF

(unrolls photo)

Oh, Claude, I love it. Hey, Claude, it's beautiful.
Hey, everybody, look what Claude gave me . . .
I love you. Oh, I love you. I'm in love with you.
I can't help it. You're terrific . . . I'm in love
with this guy, see. I like his looks to begin with.
Anybody would. Besides he has a certain spec-
tacular quality. I love him, I can't help it. I'm
not a homosexual or anything like that . . . but
I'd go to bed with him . . . and make great love
to you . . . He's the sun and I'm the earth. He's
infinite. He's got this beautiful head. He's Leo
the Lion, the only guy I'd ever go to bed with.

MICK JAGGER—Mick . . . Mickey . . . My
Mick . . . My Mickey Mick . . .

MICKEY MY MICKEY MICK
MY MICKEY JAG MICKEY JAG
MICKEY MICK MY MICKEY MICK
MY MICKEY JAG JAG
MICKEY MICK MICK
MICKEY MICK MICK
MICK MICK MY JAGGER

BERGER

(entering, followed by Sheila)

Hud, let's lock up.

HUD

Right.

> *(The band has stopped playing, The Tribe now speak in low voices, as if expecting something to happen. Hud switches off the lights. For a moment the stage is in darkness, but candles are lit. Hud locks the door.)*

SHEILA

(breaking the silence—to audience)

I'm so tired . . . I hope this doesn't take long.

CLAUDE

What did you say?

BERGER

(*wearing dark goggles, passing out sticks of marijuana to The Tribe. As he stops by each, he has a line*)

Forty-four and one-hundred-percent pure.

SHEILA

Oh . . . your movie . . . I see you're taking it with you . . .

CLAUDE

My baby . . .

BERGER

Separates the men from the boys.

SHEILA

How's it coming?

BERGER

No sticky mess.

CLAUDE

I'm almost finished with it . . .

BERGER

Jet to Miami——come on down.

SHEILA

Finished with what?

CLAUDE

My movie . . .

BERGER

That heavenly flavor.

SHEILA

Oh, yeah, how's it coming? What's Berger doing?

BERGER

Relieve headache pain fast, fast, fast.

CLAUDE

He's passing out the pot.

BERGER

Relief is just a swallow away.

CLAUDE

It's groovy for food and sex.

BERGER

Shrinks hemorrhoids.

SHEILA

All you want to do is ball.

CLAUDE

I beg your pardon.

BERGER

(*bringing the pot to Sheila and Claude*)

Only one calorie.

SHEILA

(*sarcastically to Claude*)

Have a good trip!

BERGER

(*nicely to Claude*)

Yeah, bon voyage!

CLAUDE

(*to Berger*)

Bless you, sweet child of God.

BERGER

(*to audience*)

I got my job through the Village Voice.

CLAUDE

(*to The Tribe*)

Pick up your glowworms.

(*The Tribe all light up. There is no talking now. No music. All is silent, but for the sound of The Tribe inhaling. This should be a rather significant moment. The drummer quietly begins a rocking rhythm with a snare drum and brush.*)

THE TRIBE

DOORS LOCKED
DOORS LOCKED
BLINDS PULLED
BLINDS PULLED
LIGHTS LOW
LIGHTS LOW
FLAMES HIGH
FLAMES HIGH

MY BODY
MY BODY
MY BODY

MY BODY
MY BODY
MY BODY

MY BODY
IS WALKING IN SPACE
MY SOUL IS IN ORBIT
WITH GOD, FACE TO FACE

FLOATING, FLIPPING
FLYING, TRIPPING

TRIPPING FROM POTTSVILLE
  TO MAINLINE
TRIPPING FROM MAINLINE
  TO MOONVILLE

ON A ROCKET TO THE
  FOURTH DIMENSION
TOTAL SELF-AWARENESS
  THE INTENTION

MY MIND IS CLEAR AS COUNTRY AIR
I FEEL MY FLESH, ALL COLORS MESH

RED-BLACK
BLUE-BROWN
YELLOW-CRIMSON
GREEN-ORANGE

PURPLE-PINK
VIOLET-WHITE
WHITE-WHITE
WHITE
WHITE

ALL THE CLOUDS ARE CUMULOFT
WALKING IN SPACE
OH MY GOD YOUR SKIN IS SOFT
I LOVE YOUR FACE

HOW DARE THEY TRY TO END
    THIS BEAUTY
HOW DARE THEY TRY TO END
    THIS BEAUTY

TO KEEP US UNDER FOOT
THEY BURY US IN SOOT

PRETENDING IT'S A CHORE
TO SHIP US OFF TO WAR

IN THIS DIVE
WE RE-DISCOVER SENSATION
IN THIS DIVE
WE RE-DISCOVER SENSATION

WALKING IN SPACE
WE FIND THE PURPOSE OF PEACE

THE BEAUTY OF LIFE
YOU CAN NO LONGER HIDE

OUR EYES ARE OPEN
OUR EYES ARE OPEN
OUR EYES ARE OPEN
OUR EYES ARE OPEN
WIDE WIDE WIDE

> (*Lights down on stage during last part of this song. Spot on Claude. The following is his trip.*)

GI 1 (HUD)

All right, my pretty boys. Prepare to bail out. Bail out, soldier boys. I said, skydive.

GI 2 (WOOF)

I'm not even twenty-one yet and they've got me jumping out of airplanes.

GI 1 (HUD)

Hello, White Man.

GI 2 (WOOF)

Hello, Yellow Man, down there. I'm gonna get you.

GI 1 (HUD)

(*taking Woof's hand*)

Black and white go nice together, don't they?

GI 3

We're unfrocked paratroopers.

GI 4

Home of Macrobiotics and Sanpaku.

GI 5

It just proves what I always said. There just aren't that many places to go anymore.

GI 6

The machine age is overexposing me.

GI 7

My father is sure a jerk.

GI 8 (CLAUDE)

Gee, just like the movies.

GI 9

I don't want to be anything, and I certainly don't want to be a housewife with kids.

Don't worry, you won't.

ALL THE TRIBE

I'm hanging loose.

> (*The Tribe runs off as Berger, impersonating George Washington, enters. He wears a powdered wig askew, carries a battle-worn American flag, leading a bedraggled troop of men.*)

GEORGE

> (*marching on*)

Hut two three four. Hut two three four. Jump to it, lads. Kill the Redcoats. Into the Delaware, men. Grab your muskets. For God, for Country, for Crown, for Freedom, for Liberation, for Mother . . .

MESSENGER (WOOF)

> (*running on*)

General Washington, General Washington, your highness . . . news from the front. The word is retreat. Threat of attack.

> (*George Washington hands powdered wig*)

and flag to Messenger and flees as In-
dians in loincloths with tomahawks and war
paint attack.)

INDIAN 1

White Man DIE!

INDIAN 2

Crazy Horse say, White Man DIE!

INDIAN 3

Cochise say, White Man DIE!

INDIAN 1

Geronimo say, White Man DIE!

INDIAN 2

Sitting Bull say, White Man DIE!

INDIAN 3

Little Beaver say, White Man DIE!

INDIAN 1

This INDIAN land. Oh, Manitou, Great Spirit,
White Man steal our land. White Man must die.

INDIAN 2

Many moons since Roanoke. Once again White Man comes. Queen Bess and John Smith from England make peace. Take Papoose Pocahontas. Wahunsunacook kill white man.

> (*The Indians exit in a war dance of victory. George Washington's men lie still on stage in a massacre. A bugle sounds reveille. The man playing the bugle appears wearing a Civil War Rebel uniform.*)

U. S. GRANT

> (*heavy southern drawl*)

Friends, I want you to meet a great friend of yours . . . General Grant. I have arrived. I say, General Grant is here. Hey, wake up. Come on, you guys . . . get up . . .

> (*He shakes the men and they gradually revive and get up.*)

. . . wake up . . . come on. We have to push on to Raleigh.

> (*The men fall into formation.*)

Roll Call: Abraham Lincoln.

> (*He takes a swig of whiskey.*)

ABRAHAM LINCOLN

"P"-resent, sir.

U. S. GRANT

John W. Booth.

JOHN W. BOOTH

(*Shakespearean actor*)

Evah-prrresent, sire.

(*brandishing small pistol*)

U. S. GRANT

Calvin Coolidge.

CALVIN COOLIDGE

Voh-dee-oh-doe, sir.

U. S. GRANT

Clark Gable.

CLARK GABLE (WOOF)

Yup.

U. S. GRANT

Scarlett O'Hara.

SCARLETT

(*southern accent*)

Here I am.

U. S. GRANT

(*going to kiss her*)

Why, Scarlett, honey! . . . Teddy.

TEDDY ROOSEVELT (HUD)

Right. I'm ready, giddy up.

U. S. GRANT

Colonel Custer.

COLONEL CUSTER (JEANIE)

At last.

U. S. GRANT

Claude Bukowski.

CLAUDE

He couldn't make it.

U. S. GRANT

Well, men, let's be gone. Heads up . . . shoulders

back . . . onward, Christian soldiers, to Appomatox. Forward, Harch.

> (*They dance a minuet, but are attacked from behind by a group of Negroes. Some modern day, with switch blades. Some Africans with blowguns and spears, dressed as natives in feathers, etc., some dirty, poor slaves. African drums in background. The Negroes confront the whites.*)

AFRICAN WITCH DOCTOR

> (*carrying spear*)

Walla walla
Goona goona
Miobie
Manatoga
Gooba Gooba
Voodoo Waba

LE ROI JONES (HUD)

> (*carries a banner "Black Power" and a switchblade knife*)

I cut yo' up. I hate you and your white mothers. I hope you all die and rot. You're all for shit.

> (*The Negroes attack and kill the white soldiers.*)

SLAVE

(standing over the dead bodies, with his foot on Abraham Lincoln's chest, very happy)

Yes, I'm finished on y'all's farm land. With yo' boll weevils and all, and pluckin' y'all's chickens, fryin' mother's oats in grease. I'm free now, thanks to yo', Massa Lincoln, emancipator of the slave. Yeah! Emancimotherfuckin'-pator of the slave.

(The Negroes sing together.)

THE NEGROES

HAPPY BIRTHDAY, ABIE BABY
HAPPY BIRTHDAY TO YOU . . .

(Suddenly the stage becomes a battlefield. War sound effects up loud. Plus electronic music in the background. They exit in fright.

Four Buddhist Monks enter in long saffron robes, kneeling down front. The first Monk pours gasoline over himself from a can.)

BUDDHIST MONK 1

Use High Octane and feel the tiger in your tank.

(He lights a wad of flash paper, dies an agonizing death, lies in a heap on the stage.)

BUDDHIST MONK 2

Everyone should be Buddha.

BUDDHIST MONK 3

We are all one.

BUDDHIST MONK 4

No more war toys.

BUDDHIST MONK 2

Hustling is an honest profession.

(*Three Catholic nuns enter behind praying Buddhists.*)

THE NUNS

Hail, Mary, full of Grace, blessed is the fruit of the loom.

(*They strangle the Buddhists with their rosary beads.*)

Holy Mary, Mother of God, pray for us sinners, now and at the hour of our death . . .

(*Three astronauts enter behind the Nuns, killing them with ray guns. Three Chinese enter behind the astronauts, carrying machine guns, killing the astronauts. Four*

American Indians, with war yelps, kill the Chinese with tomahawks. Two Green Berets with machine guns kill the Indians and each other. All the bodies lie in a heap as a strobe light flashes on. The killing scene goes into reverse now, all the bodies coming back to life, exiting backward and reentering at a faster pace to go through the exact killing ritual two more times, each time at a still faster pace. At the end, all the sound and strobe lights off, leaving the bodies in a silent, motionless heap.

One by one the bodies rise in slow motion, as others sing.)

THE TRIBE

(perhaps prerecorded)

RIPPED OPEN BY METAL EXPLOSION
CAUGHT IN BARBED WIRE
FIREBALL
BULLET SHOCK
BAYONET ELECTRICITY
SHRAPNELLED
THROBBING MEAT
ELECTRONIC DATA PROCESSING
BLACK UNIFORMS
BARE FEET

CARBINES
MAIL-ORDER RIFLES
SHOOT THE MUSCLES
256 VIETCONG CAPTURED
256 VIETCONG CAPTURED

(*live—the whole Tribe singing*)

PRISONERS IN NIGGERTOWN
IT'S A DIRTY LITTLE WAR
THREE FIVE ZERO ZERO
TAKE WEAPONS UP AND BEGIN TO KILL
WATCH THE LONG LONG ARMIES
  DRIFTING HOME

(*into a joyous march*)

PRISONERS IN NIGGERTOWN
IT'S A DIRTY LITTLE WAR
THREE FIVE ZERO ZERO
TAKE WEAPONS UP AND BEGIN TO KILL
WATCH THE LONG LONG ARMIES
  DRIFTING HOME

(*settling back down on the floor, as at the
beginning of "Walking in Space"*)

HOW DARE THEY TRY TO END
  THIS BEAUTY
HOW DARE THEY TRY TO END
  THIS BEAUTY

WALKING IN SPACE
WE FIND THE PURPOSE OF PEACE
THE BEAUTY OF LIFE
   YOU CAN NO LONGER HIDE

OUR EYES ARE OPEN
OUR EYES ARE OPEN
OUR EYES ARE OPEN
OUR EYES ARE OPEN

   (*lights down, spot on Claude as at beginning of war sequence*)

WIDE
WIDE
WIDE

   (*stage in darkness but for spot on Claude with his eyes closed. He opens his eyes, stands slowly, not knowing where he is for a moment.*)

CLAUDE

Berger . . . George.

   (*All The Tribe on stage prostrate, as if asleep.*)

BERGER

   (*sits up*)

I'm zonked.

(Claude rushes over to Berger, sits next to him, looks at Berger, The Tribe, and the audience.)

CLAUDE

What a piece of work is man. How noble in reason, how infinite in faculties, in form and moving how express and admirable, in action how like an angel.

BERGER

In apprehension how like a god . . .

BERGER *and* CLAUDE

(together)

The beauty of the world, the paragon of animals.

CLAUDE

I have of late—but wherefore I know not—lost all my mirth . . . this goodly frame, the earth, seems to me a sterile promontory, this most excellent canopy, the air, look you, this brave o'erhanging firmament, this majestical roof fretted with golden fire, why, it appears no other thing to me than a foul and pestilent congregation of vapours.

BERGER

Claude . . .

CLAUDE

What?

BERGER

I feel lonely already, Claude.

> (*They look at each other for a moment, Berger moves to Claude, puts his arm around Claude. Claude makes no response.*)

CLAUDE

Start facing reality . . . sometimes I think I'm going crazy . . . out of mind . . . maybe cancer on the brain or something . . .

BERGER

Maybe the Army is the best place for you . . . let them keep you, sleep you, feed you. I'm putting you on, Claude.

CLAUDE

I'm not going into the Army tomorrow!

BERGER

I know.

CLAUDE

Let's go to Mexico, George.

BERGER

I told you the *boogey man* would get you.

CLAUDE

I want to eat mushrooms and sleep in the sun.

BERGER

O.K. Let's go. I'll go with you.

CLAUDE

I know where it's at.

BERGER

You know where it's at.

CLAUDE

You know where it's at.

BERGER

I know where it's at.

CLAUDE

I can't live like this anymore. I'm not happy.

It's too difficult, I can't open myself up like that. I can't make this moment to moment living on the streets.

BERGER

I dig it.

CLAUDE

I don't.

BERGER

Putting on his peace paint he said: On with the groovy revolution.

CLAUDE

I don't want to be a dentist or a lawyer or a bum or an IBM machine. I don't want to be a rock 'n' roll hero or a movie star. I just want to have lots of money.

BERGER

I'm gonna go to India . . . float around . . . live in little huts in Beirut . . . feed the poor Indians in a little village somewhere . . . like Albert Schweitzer . . . bake bread. I'm gonna stay high forever. They'll never get me. I'm gonna stay high forever.

CLAUDE

I'll tell you the thing I'd really like to be . . .
invisible. I don't need drugs. An invisible man,
and I could fly and see into people's minds and
know what they're thinking . . . I could do anything, go anywhere, and be happy . . . not tied
down to a stupid job or anybody. And I could
perform miracles. That's the only thing I'd like
to do or be on this dirt.

BERGER

Then you're the King of Wands.

CLAUDE

Shazam!

(*He tries to fly.*)

Oh, my God, it's one o'clock. I have to be at the
station at 8:30.

BERGER

Claude, they've sucked you in.

CLAUDE

They've fucked me.

BERGER

I hate the fuckin' world, don't you.

CLAUDE

I hate the fuckin' world, I hate the fuckin' winter, I hate these fuckin' streets.

BERGER

I wish the fuck it would snow at least.

CLAUDE

I wish it was the biggest fucking snowstorm. Blizzards, come down in sheets, mountains, rivers, oceans, forests, rabbits, cover everything in beautiful, white, holy snow, and I could hide out a hermit and hang on a cross and eat cornflakes.

BERGER

A fucking blizzard.

CLAUDE

Oh, fuck.

BERGER

Oh, fuckey, fuck, fuck.

CLAUDE

(*to audience*)

I was in the shower this morning and I reached

down and I couldn't find it . . . it fell off and washed down the drain.

BERGER

Anybody see it, anybody see this little thing? Sheila, did you see it? Claude lost this little thing, about this big . . .

(*He goes to Sheila and helps her up.*)

Sheila, how come you're so groovy looking tonight? You've got fab eyes.

SHEILA

(*shaking him off*)

Come off it, Iceberger.

CLAUDE

(*coming over*)

Sheila, you're not mad at me, are you?

SHEILA

No, why should I be mad?

CLAUDE

Well, let's all go someplace . . . get coffee . . .

WOOF

I'm tired, I'm going home . . .

BERGER

We're going up to Sheila's pad. Aren't we, Sheila?

> (*Focus now centers on Woof, Jeanie, Crissy, Charlie, Sharon. As each talks he helps the other up.*)

WOOF

Jeanie, you want to come with me?

JEANIE

Disappear, Shrimpboats.

> (*She walks away.*)

WOOF

O.K. How about you, Crissy? You wanna come?

CRISSY

No, not tonight, I'm comin' with Charlie, ain't I, Charlie?

CHARLIE

I don't care.

(*to Sharon*)

Is it all right, Sharon, if Crissy comes with us?

SHARON

We slept together last week. I'd rather sleep alone together.

CRISSY

What about me?

WOOF

(*to Crissy*)

How about me?

CRISSY

Too little, tobacco breath.

CHARLIE

(*to Crissy*)

Look, I don't care . . .

(*to Sharon*)

It's all the same thing, isn't it?

(*Crissy and Sharon both walk away from Charlie, Crissy moving over to Dionne.*)

WOOF

See ya', Charlie.

(*moves away*)

I'm going home to finish the Bible.

CHARLIE

(*standing alone*)

Hey, wait a minute . . .

(*Charlie follows Sharon upstage.*

Focus shifts to other side of stage—Dennis, Bob, Dick.)

DENNIS

(*to Dick*)

Just come over to my pad, baby . . .

DICK

Eat your own sperm.

BOB

Let's go down to the docks for cocks.

DICK

Aw, go get married!

WOOF

Everybody, if we all sleep together, it'll be nice and warm . . .

(*Focus shifts to Jeanie, Dionne, and Crissy.*)

JEANIE

(*to Dionne*)

I don't want to sleep with *that*.

DIONNE

(*to Crissy*)

All right, then, you sleep with it.

CRISSY

Me? Never happen.

WOOF

Hey, Helen, I'll walk you home, Helen.

HELEN

Walk to Hoboken?

(*Focus now to include Claude, Berger, Sheila, Dionne, Woof*)

JEANIE

(*moving to Claude*)

I'll sleep with *you* if you want me to. Do you?

CLAUDE

Boring . . .

(*turning to Sheila*)

Sheila, I'd like to go to bed with you.

SHEILA

Why?

CLAUDE

Because I like you.

LOUISE

(*skinny girl*)

Woof, I'd like to take a bath with you.

WOOF

Ahhhh! I'm Catholic!

BERGER

(*Organizing Claude, Sheila, Hud, Dionne, Woof*)

Com'on, Com'on . . .

WOOF

Sheila, will you marry me?

JEANIE

I wanna go too.
(*She tags along.*)

HUD

Oh . . . we're gonna go Ubangi . . .

BERGER

To Sheila's pad . . .

JEANIE

Go, go, Ubangi . . .

DIONNE

Bang bang.
Gang bang.
Bang gang.
Bugaloo-a-boo-boo.

WOOF

Yeah, yeah, com'on, everybody, bang bang . . .

SHEILA

(*looking at the sky*)

GOOD MORNING STARSHINE
THE EARTH SAYS HELLO
YOU TWINKLE ABOVE US
WE TWINKLE BELOW

(*Dionne joins Sheila.*)

DIONNE *and* SHEILA

(*looking at the sky*)

GOOD MORNING STARSHINE
YOU LEAD US ALONG
MY LOVE AND ME
AS WE SING OUR
EARLY MORNING SINGING SONG

GLIDDY GLUP GLOOPY
NIBBY NABBY NOOPY
LA LA—LO LO

CLAUDE, BERGER, WOOF, HUD

SABBA SIBBY SABBA
NOOBY ABA NABA
LE LE—LO LO

TOOBY OOBY WALA
NOOBY ABA NABA

EARLY MORNING
SINGING SONG

GOOD MORNING STARSHINE
THE EARTH SAYS HELLO
YOU TWINKLE ABOVE US
WE TWINKLE BELOW

GOOD MORNING STARSHINE
YOU LEAD US ALONG
MY LOVE AND ME
AS WE SING OUR
EARLY MORNING SINGING SONG

GLIDDY GLUP GLOOPY
NIBBY NABBY NOOPY
LA LA—LO LO

ALL

TOOBY OOBY WALA
NOOBY ABA NABA

EARLY MORNING
SINGING SONG

SINGING A SONG
HUMMING A SONG
SINGING A SONG
LOVING A SONG
LAUGHING A SONG
SING THE SONG
SING THE SONG
SONG SONG SONG SING
SING SING SING SONG

MAN

Shut up down there! We want to get some sleep!
Scum bags!

BERGER

(*climbing partway up the Crucifix-Tree*)

Behold, he said, with a wave toward the harbor, see the magnificent ocean . . . Italy, Spain, Switzerland, Russia, and, yes, Claude's England.

HUD

(*reading from a National Enquirer*)

"Learn How Twenty-seven Die in Acid."

SHEILA

Sheila's hands, George's feet, and Claude's poor little brain matter more than the whole sweep of those damned constellations.

WOMAN

Shut up! We're trying to sleep. We have to go to work in the morning, Flag Burners!

CLAUDE

Cosmic Fart!

BERGER

(*shouting*)

I ride into Infinitude on the top of Manhateeny Island.

SHEILA

God has hands like mine and feet like yours and Claude's brain.

HUD

"Youth Threatens to Drop LSD in New York City Reservoir."

BERGER

Save me God from Infinity.

HUD

GM gets rich, GI's die.

SHEILA

Without God, we'd be no more than bacteria breeding on a pebble in space.

BERGER

Blah! to the immensity of space.

HUD

"Man Gives Address as Heaven Six Hours Before Plane Crashes."

MAN *and* WOMAN

(*from up above*)

Shut up down there, for God's sake, we want to get some sleep, etc.

CLAUDE

(*shouting at Man and Woman*)

I am the Son of God . . .

MAN

Oh, yeah, New York is a rat's ass.

WOMAN

(*correcting him*)

New York is a Winter Festival. Blah!

CLAUDE

(*quietly*)

I am the Son of God.

BERGER

(*shouting*)

Blah! to the electric universe.

CLAUDE

I will vanish and be forgotten.

(quiet reprise: "Good Morning Starshine")

SHEILA

(looking at the sky)

LOOK AT THE MOON
LOOK AT THE MOON
LOOK AT THE MOON
LOOK AT THE MOON
LOOK AT THE MOON
LOOK AT THE MOON
LOOK AT THE MOON

GOOD MORNING STARSHINE
THE EARTH SAYS HELLO
YOU TWINKLE ABOVE US
WE TWINKLE BELOW

DIONNE *and* JEANIE

(joining Sheila)

GOOD MORNING STARSHINE
YOU LEAD US ALONG
MY LOVE AND ME
AS WE SING
OUR EARLY MORNING SINGING SONG

GLIDDY GLUP GLOOPY
NIBBY NABBY NOOPY
LA LA LA LO LO

CLAUDE, BERGER, WOOF, HUD

(*joining in*)

SABBA SIBBY SABBA
NOOBY ABA NABA
LE LE LO LO

TOOBY OOBY WALA
NOOBY ABA NABA

EARLY MORNING SINGING SONG

(*All The Tribe join on a repeat of this lyric.*

As they sing, the relationships of the principals should be very evident: Dionne and Hud together; Jeanie and Woof, each separate, almost outsiders, but each with so much love to give; Sheila very aware of the situation now, still very much hung up on Berger, yet liking Claude; Claude in love with Sheila, but of course having no idea of what is in store for him, very aware he will soon be leaving all this; Berger realizing how close it is to Claude's departure and trying to be happy-go-lucky in spite of his feelings.

Some of The Tribe are bringing in the mattresses from off.)

THE TRIBE

Look what we found!

> (*This song starts as a chant.*)

UUUUUUUUUUUUUUUUU THE BED
AAAAAAAAAAAAAAAA THE BED
UUUUUUUUUUUUUUUGH THE BED
OH THE BED
MMMMMMM THE BED
I LOVE THE BED

> (*During the following they manipulate the
> mattresses, put on psychedelic sheets, pil-
> lows, flower petals, and end by placing
> Claude and Sheila on the bed side by side.*)

YOU CAN LIE IN BED
YOU CAN LAY IN BED
YOU CAN DIE IN BED
YOU CAN PRAY IN BED

YOU CAN LIVE IN BED
YOU CAN LAUGH IN BED
YOU CAN GIVE YOUR HEART
OR BREAK YOUR HEART
  IN HALF IN BED

YOU CAN TEASE IN BED
YOU CAN PLEASE IN BED
YOU CAN SQUEEZE IN BED
YOU CAN FREEZE IN BED

YOU CAN SNEEZE IN BED
CATCH THE FLEAS IN BED
ALL OF THESE
PLUS EAT CRACKERS AND CHEESE
  IN BED

   OH THE BED IS A THING
   OF FEATHER AND SPRING
   OF WIRE AND WOOD
   INVENTION SO GOOD

   OH THE BED COMES COMPLETE
   WITH PILLOW AND SHEET
   WITH BLANKET ELECTRIC
   AND BREATH ANTISEPTIC

   LET THERE BE SHEETS
   LET THERE BE BEDS
   FOAM RUBBER PILLOWS
   UNDER OUR HEADS

   LET THERE BE SIGHS
   FILLING THE ROOM
   SCANTY PAJAMAS
   BY FRUIT OF THE LOOM

YOU CAN EAT IN BED
YOU CAN BEAT IN BED
BE IN HEAT IN BED
HAVE A TREAT IN BED

YOU CAN ROCK IN BED
YOU CAN ROLL IN BED
FIND YOUR COCK IN BED
LOSE YOUR SOUL IN BED

YOU CAN LOSE IN BED
YOU CAN WIN IN BED
BUT NEVER NEVER NEVER NEVER
NEVER NEVER NEVER NEVER
NEVER NEVER NEVER
NEVER CAN YOU SIN IN BED

NEVER SIN IN BED

> (*As the song ends, The Tribe have placed Claude and Sheila side by side on the bed and exit—or stand forming walls of the room.*
>
> *Hold on the image of Claude and Sheila side by side on the bed, then*)

SHEILA

(*getting up, running to door*)

Berger . . . Berger.

CLAUDE

Oh, did Berger go? . . . I'll go too.

(*starting to get up*)

SHEILA

No, you can stay.

CLAUDE

Stay?

SHEILA

Stay for coffee.

CLAUDE

O.K., coffee!

(*Sheila goes off to make coffee, Claude stands on bed, takes bow out of his hair, combs hair, as Jeanie runs on, tackling Claude, they fall on the bed.*)

JEANIE

Claude, what time does your train leave?

CLAUDE

Jeanie . . . you left!

JEANIE

Oh . . . I won't be able to make the train, Claude. I'm gonna get killed when I get home . . . so, can I say good-bye now?

(*Jeanie is on top of Claude as Sheila enters holding two burning sticks of incense.*)

SHEILA

Hi, Jeanie.

JEANIE

Hi, Sheila.

CLAUDE

Beat it, Jeanie.

JEANIE

Yeah, yeah, yeah . . . aw, Claude, I just love you, that's all. Don't mind me.

CLAUDE

Jeanie, please.

JEANIE

I'm going, don't worry.

(*getting up from the bed*)

Claude, I want you to have a great time, Claude. You're a great guy. You're sweet.

CLAUDE

You're sweet too, Jeanie. Beat it.

JEANIE

So long, love.

(*exits.*

long pause as Claude and Sheila take in their situation)

SHEILA

You're standing on my bed.

CLAUDE

(*not moving*)

Thank you. It's beautiful.

SHEILA

Well?

CLAUDE

Well?

(*Sheila sits on bed, lotus position, holding two burning sticks of incense.*)

SHEILA

My pad is the crossroads of a thousand private lives. Why don't you sit down?

CLAUDE

(*sitting*)

He sits.

SHEILA

Do you want some incense?

CLAUDE

(*taking a stick*)

No.

SHEILA

Well?

CLAUDE

Well?

SHEILA

Relax!

CLAUDE

(*falling back on the bed*)

He relaxes.

SHEILA

Where did Berger go?

CLAUDE

Why don't *you* relax?

SHEILA

Claude, I'm the hippest . . .

CLAUDE

Don't you love me?

SHEILA

. . . I know your problem.

CLAUDE

(*sitting up*)

Have pity on your poor war baby.

(*Claude touches Sheila's arm.*)

SHEILA

(*violent reaction—She gets up from the
bed.*)

I'll scream bloody murder if you touch me, Daddy Warbucks!

CLAUDE

What?

SHEILA

. . . You lay a pinky on my *titty* and they'll hear about it all over the *city*.

CLAUDE

Oh, you're a Liverpool poet.

SHEILA

I'm sorry, Claude . . . I can't do it . . . I'm so upset . . . I'm so mixed up . . .

CLAUDE

I'm not asking you to do anything.

SHEILA

It's not you who's asking.

CLAUDE

I'm not gonna bite you . . . unless you ask me to . . .

SHEILA

I'm sorry, Berger.

(*Claude hears her mistake.*)

CLAUDE

Sheila . . . I'd like to tell you something that I've never told to anyone else. Not even Berger. But I don't know if you're strong enough to take it.

SHEILA

What do you mean?

CLAUDE

Sit down.

SHEILA

(*sitting on floor, next to bed*)

She sits.

CLAUDE

Now, please, Sheila, you must believe me, and promise me you won't get frightened or anything.

SHEILA

I don't know what you're talking about. What do you mean?

CLAUDE

Well, you see, Sheila . . . I come from another planet.

SHEILA

Oh, yeah? I'm leaving . . .

> (*getting up to move away, Claude grabs her hand.*)

CLAUDE

Yeah, it's true. Just look at my eyes. I have been sent to Earth on a mission. There are many others here like me. We're observing you.

SHEILA

Another scene from your Walt Disney movie?

CLAUDE

Believe me, it's true . . . please don't make fun of me. I'm from another planet in another galaxy.

SHEILA

What's your planet called?

CLAUDE

What's it called?

SHEILA

What's it called?

CLAUDE

Explanezanetooch.

SHEILA

What?

CLAUDE

Exanaplanetooch.

SHEILA

Nice name.

CLAUDE

You believe me?

SHEILA

Of course.

CLAUDE

Can I tell you about it?

SHEILA

Of course, I'm dying to hear about it.

CLAUDE

No, I don't think I can . . . I shouldn't have
told you . . . you don't believe me . . .

SHEILA

I believe you, believe me, I believe you . . . I
always knew there was something strange about
you . . . you come from another planet . . .

CLAUDE

EXANAPLANETOOCH
A PLANET IN ANOTHER GALAXY
EXANAPLANETOOCH
A PLACE WHERE ALL THE PEOPLE
   LOOK LIKE ME

A PLANET WHERE THE AIR IS PURE
THE RIVER WATERS CRYSTAL BRIGHT
THE SKY IS GREEN
AND IN THE NIGHT
TWELVE GOLDEN MOONS
PROVIDE THE LIGHT

THE BUILDINGS IN THE CITIES
SHAPED LIKE HILLS
MADE OF BLACK AND GREEN
AND BLUE AND YELLOW GLASS
WITH RIVERS RUNNING THROUGH
   THEM
CRYSTAL BRIGHT

SWIM IN THE WATER
DRINK FROM THE RIVERS
TOTAL BEAUTY TOTAL HEALTH
EV'RYMAN'S AN ARTIST
   AND A SCIENTIST-PHILOSOPHER
NO GOVERNMENT AND NO POLICE
NO WARS NO CRIME NO HATE
JUST HAPPINESS AND LOVE

FULFILLMENT OF EACH MAN'S
   POTENTIAL
AND AMBITION
WITH EVER-WIDENING HORIZONS

EXANAPLANETOOCH
A PLANET IN ANOTHER GALAXY
EXANAPLANETOOCH
WOULD YOU LIKE TO GO BACK
   WITH ME

     (*music continues under*)

Sheila, I'm not going into the Army tomorrow.
My people are sending a space ship for me
and I'm going back to my home. Will you come
with me?

SHEILA

It would be exciting, wouldn't it?

(crawling toward Claude)

EXANAPLANETOOCH

CLAUDE

EXANAPLANETOOCH

SHEILA

I'll leave a note for my parents.

CLAUDE *and* SHEILA

EXANAPLANETOOCH

> *(They go down on the bed together, Claude on top of Sheila, kissing her.*
>
> *Lights fade. Spotlight on them throbs a little and goes out.*
>
> *In the blackout, the bed is carried off, as we hear The Girls' voices:)*

THE GIRLS

SENTIMENTAL ENDING
SENTIMENTAL ENDING
SENTIMENTAL ENDING
SENTIMENTAL ENDING
etc.

> *(spotlight up on Sheila)*

SHEILA

I REACHED IT
HE REACHED IT
YOU REACHED IT
WE ALL REACHED THE CLIMAX

I LOVED IT
HE LOVED IT
YOU LOVED IT
WE ALL LOVED THE CLIMAX

FASTEN YOUR SEATBELTS
HANG ON UP-TIGHT
APPROACHING FOR LANDING
AND EVERYTHING TURNS OUT
   DELIGHTFULLY RIGHT

I'VE HAD IT
HE'S HAD IT
YOU'VE HAD IT
WE'VE ALL HAD THE CLIMAX

THIS IS THE TURNING POINT

FUNNY
BUT BY THE END
BITTER AND SERIOUS AND DEADLY

(*Lights up behind Sheila on The Guys in*

file at attention, in full Army battle dress, steel helmets, back packs, etc. They join Sheila)

THE GUYS

I'VE HAD IT

SHEILA

I'VE HAD IT

THE GUYS

HE'S HAD IT

SHEILA

HE'S HAD IT

THE GUYS

YOU'VE HAD IT

SHEILA

YOU'VE HAD IT

THE GUYS *and* SHEILA

WE'VE ALL HAD THE CLIMAX
THE CLIMAX
THE CLIMAX

SHEILA

THIS IS THE TURNING POINT

(*Sheila exits.*

Lights up full)

THE SOLDIERS

(*viciously exaggerated and rapid military maneuvers*)

Right Face. Left Face. In Place March. About Face. Parade Rest. Attention. Left Face. Right Face. Double Time March, etc.

(*They freeze at attention.*

Mom and Dad enter, carrying a man's suit on a hanger with a mask. This represents their son. They stand center, both looking at the suit of clothes which Dad holds between them.)

MOM

(*kissing the mask*)

Momma loves you.

DAD

(*goes to kiss mask, but pulls back, shakes arm of suitcoat*)

I've waited a long time for this day.

MOM

(*kisses mask*)

Now write me a letter tonight.

DAD

(*starts to kiss, pulls back, shakes the empty sleeve*)

You don't know how proud I am of you, son, today.

MOM

(*kisses mask*)

Give us a kiss.

(*kisses mask*)

DAD

(*shakes the empty sleeve and puts money into coat pocket*)

Be a man.

(*They walk him over to The Guys and hand suit to one of The Guys. Mom and Dad stand to one side.*

Berger enters, calling to Sheila.)

BERGER

Sheila . . . Sheila . . . over here . . .

(*Sheila enters from opposite direction. She wears Claude's white sari with a sash. Berger hugs her affectionately. She makes no response. He backs away, reacting to this and really seeing for the first time that Sheila is wearing Claude's sari.*)

BERGER

Sheila, we thought you were gonna miss the train.

WOOF

Where's Claude?

BERGER

Yeah, where is he?

SHEILA

He's here. He's here. He's embarrassed.

BERGER

Embarrassed? About what?

SHEILA

You'll see.

BERGER

Listen, the train's leaving.

DAD

All Aboard!

> (*Someone imitates a train whistle.*)

SHEILA

> (*calling off*)

Claude . . .

> (*Claude approaching, not yet in view*)

BERGER

Claude, what did you do to yourself?

> (*Claude enters, almost in shock; he wears a dark sweater, dark slacks, a navy knit stocking cap, carries his bag and the movie script.*)

CLAUDE

Berger . . . I feel like I died.

BERGER

What happened, Claudio?

CLAUDE

I . . . I . . .

SHEILA

I cut his hair off . . . he asked me to . . .

CLAUDE

I didn't want them to get it. Here, George, I want you to have it.

> (*He hands Berger a paper sack, his shorn hair inside.*)

BERGER

> (*looking at package*)

Oh, Claude . . . Claude . . .

CLAUDE

Keep it for me. Maybe I can have a wig made when I get out.

BERGER

Claude . . . I . . .

CLAUDE

Don't anybody say anything . . .

DAD

(transformed into a sergeant)

Irish.

SOLDIER 1

Present, sir.

DAD

Italian.

SOLDIER 2

Present, sir.

DAD

Jew.

SOLDIER 3

Here, sir.

DAD

German.

SOLDIER 4

Present, sir.

DAD

English.

SOLDIER 5

Yo! sir.

DAD

Puerto Rican.

SOLDIER 6

Present, sir.

DAD

Polish.
> (*no response*)

Claude Bukowski.
> (*no response*)

Claude Bukowski.

CLAUDE

> (*joins the file of men, then answers*)

Present, sir.

DAD

Left Face.
> (*The Soldiers—"the train"—do a left face.*)

MOM

Where's a taxi? . . . Service is terrible . . . I want
to get home . . .

DAD

(*no longer the sergeant*)

I guess maybe we have to take the subway . . .

MOM

Oh, I'm so tired . . .

DAD

Let's take the subway . . .

MOM

You take the subway. When I get home, I'm
going to soak in that tub . . .

(*The Soldier-Train begins to move in an
ominous, funeral march tempo.*)

THE TRIBE

SENTIMENTAL ENDING
SENTIMENTAL ENDING
SENTIMENTAL ENDING
SENTIMENTAL ENDING

SENTIMENTAL ENDING
    RIPPED OPEN BY METAL EXPLOSION
SENTIMENTAL ENDING
    CAUGHT IN BARBED WIRE
SENTIMENTAL ENDING
    FIREBALL
    BULLET SHOCK
SENTIMENTAL ENDING
    BAYONET ELECTRICITY
SENTIMENTAL ENDING
    SHRAPNELLED
    THROBBING MEAT
SENTIMENTAL ENDING
    ELECTRONIC DATA PROCESSING
SENTIMENTAL ENDING
    BLACK UNIFORMS
    BARE FEET
    CARBINES
SENTIMENTAL ENDING
    MAIL-ORDER RIFLES
    SHOOT THE MUSCLES
    256 VIETCONG CAPTURED
SENTIMENTAL ENDING
SENTIMENTAL ENDING
SENTIMENTAL ENDING
SENTIMENTAL ENDING

(The Train circles the stage in the funeral march tempo as the "Sentimental Ending"

rhythm accelerates in contrast. The Train exits, leaving Berger, Sheila, and Woof. Berger goes to Sheila, takes her hand. She looks at him and leaves. Berger stands motionless, holding the bag of Claude's hair, as Woof comes over to join him. Woof grabs hold of his yellow satin shirt. Lights fade.

"Sentimental Ending" at a furious pace in background, as if a train is racing away)

Produced by Joseph Papp and directed by Gerald Freedman, the New York Shakespeare Festival's production of **Hair** opened at the Public Theater Off-Broadway in New York on October 7, 1967, for a limited engagement of eight weeks. This "tribal love-rock musical" was hailed by the critics and public alike, not only as a stunning stride forward in the art of musical theater, but also as brilliant entertainment.

Unwilling to let his hirsute hit expire, Joseph Papp (in collaboration with Michael Butler), moved **Hair** to a large discotheque on Broadway for another run, limited by the fact that the building was about to be torn down.

Subsequently, **Hair** was revised by the authors and composer. Restaged for Broadway by Tom O'Horgan, **Hair** has enjoyed phenomenal popularity and success in New York, as well as Los Angeles, London, Paris, Copenhagen, Stockholm, Munich, Belgrade, and Sydney. Subsequent productions in a half dozen other countries are being prepared and a film version will probably be produced before 1972.